THE SPORTING LIFE

THE SPORTING LIFE
A PASSION FOR HUNTING AND FISHING

Text by Laurence Sheehan
with Carol Sama Sheehan and Kathryn George
Photographs by William Stites

CLARKSON POTTER/PUBLISHERS
NEW YORK

Published by Clarkson Potter/Publishers
201 East 50th Street
New York, New York 10022
Member of the Crown Publishing Group.

CLARKSON N. POTTER, POTTER,
and colophon are trademarks of
Clarkson N. Potter, Inc.

Manufactured in Japan

Library of Congress Cataloging-in-Publication
Data

Sheehan, Laurence.
   The sporting life: a passion for hunting and
fishing/Laurence Sheehan, Carol Sama Sheehan,
Kathryn George; photographs by William Stites.
—1st ed.
   Includes index.
   1. Hunting—United States.   2. Fishing—
United States.   3. Outdoor life—United States.
4. Hunting—United States—Pictorial works.
5. Fishing—United States—Pictorial works.
6. Outdoor life—United States—Pictorial works.
I. Sheehan, Carol Sama.   II. George, Kathryn.
III. Title.
SK41.S54   1992
799'.0973—dc20   91-37546
                                                 CIP

ISBN 0-517-58166-3

10 9 8 7 6 5 4 3 2 1

First Edition

ACKNOWLEDGMENTS

One Sunday afternoon in the fall of 1989, we piled into photographer Bill Stites' station wagon and drove to Bedford, New York, to call, unannounced, on a certain Hoagy Carmichael.

We had learned from an article he wrote on fish decoys in *Antiques* that Hoagy made bamboo fly rods, and we thought his workshop might be interesting to photograph. When we got to Hoagy's driveway, we pushed Kathy George out of the car first— because she is the smallest—and made her ring the bell. Hoagy was in the middle of a phone call, but he invited her in and went back to his office. Kathy signaled to us to join her, so by the time Hoagy returned to his living room, not one but four total strangers awaited him.

Slightly taken aback, he missed a beat, then said, "Well, would anyone like a beer?"

Carmichael's graciousness in receiving us in his home, and the two hours we spent there discussing our project and listening to his ideas and observations, proved to be typical of the welcome and cooperation we received in the two years it took to complete the research and photography for this book. If we learned nothing else, we found the devotees of fishing, hunting, and shooting, as these activities are carried on in the best traditions of each sport, to be men and women of passion, intelligence, and goodwill.

We would like to thank the following people for their assistance and encouragement (and we beg those we have overlooked to forgive the inevitable lapses):

Don Johnson and Alanna Fisher of the American Museum of Fly Fishing; Jim Brown for helping us better understand the angling experience; Judith and Jim Bowman for introducing us to the rich world of angling books; Ian Mackay and Nick Lyons of the Anglers' Club; Cathy and Barry Beck of Fishing Creek Outfitters; Miranda and David Kettlewell for educating us about the differences in the sporting life in this country and Britain; Chris Cook; Romi and Leigh Perkins for sharing their vast knowledge of the sporting world with us; Nick Bickison for taking the time to show us around some of Pennsylvania's famed trout waters; Dave Brown, John Beck, Ned Leeming, Art Chesmore; Dr. Rodolphe Coigney for letting us peek at his monumental Izaak Walton book collection; Dr. and Mrs. Alan Fried of the Catskill Fly Fishing Center; Joan Wulff and the late Lee Wulff for giving generously of their time; Poul Jorgensen, Bob Lang, Alan Liu; Susan Popkin for several valuable phone conversations; Pamela Bates Richards; Ellen and Arthur Stern for dropping us encouraging notes; Larry Stark for dropping by; Dick Tailleur and Brian McGrath.

Donal O'Brien for introducing us to his superb collection, and to Warren Gilker and carver Cigar Daisey; Roy Kroll, Peter Hitchcock, and Dickson L. Whitney for permitting us to visit two of America's historic duck clubs; Cap'n Smith, Sallie Sullivan, and her Labs; Virginia and Robin Elverson; Charlie and Jeanie Chapin for their hospitality and astute comments on the quail plantation tradition; Peter and Lillian Corbin, Karen and Tim Bontecue, Sandy and Melissa Proctor, all for treating us so kindly on several visits; Tom Daly, whose artistry and friendliness were well worth an eight-hour auto journey; Tania and Tom Evans who received us warmly in the East and West; Richard Johns for helping us illuminate the important role of sporting dogs; Winston Churchill for his early support of our project and for giving us impromptu shooting lessons on his back porch; Mickey Loudermilk for her Southern hospitality; Ralph Bufano of the Ward Museum of Wildfowl Art; Ron Hickman and Marty Kline; Pat Hornberger; John Lennon for sharing his sporting library with us; Edward Lowndes of Bluff Plantation in Charleston; O. J. Small and Tony Merck also of Charleston; Diane Jones of the John L. Wehle Gallery of Sporting Art; Rob Moir of the Peabody Museum of Salem; Jack Parker for his informed words on the art of decoy making; Don and Stephanie Palmer of Blueberry Hill Farm in Maine; Dr. Loy S. Harrell of Hawks Nest; Tommy Strange of the Santee Coastal Reserve; Hilly Thompson of Gillionville Plantation; Jimmy Vaughan of Foxfire Plantation, and Richard Wolters, dog trainer extraordinaire.

Shirley Dixon Morgan for making possible a delightful visit to the Chagrin Valley Hunt Club; Feli and Oakleigh Thorne for repeated acts of generosity and friendship; Betsy Parks for giving us insight into the life of a pack of foxhounds; George Deane, for a fascinating tour of the Eastern Shore; Wilbur R. Hubbard; Joseph B. Wiley, Jr., and Merrill and Lynda Wideman for kindly permitting our visit to the National Beagle Club; Dr. Joseph Kitchens and his staff at Pebble Hill Foundation; Peter Winants of *The Chronicle of the Horse;* Judith Ozment of the National Sporting Library; Chuck Pinnell, and Erskine and Nancy Bedford for making our stay in Middleburg so productive and so much fun; Barry and CeCe Kieselstein-Cord; Turner Reuter, Jr., and Dr. Arie M. Rijke of the Waldingfield Beagles.

Bambi Litchfield for entertaining us in high style in the Adirondacks; Kathy Blanchard of the Labrador Quebec Foundation; Len Lapsys and Ron Coffin of Brandy Brook; Sumner Crosby, Jr., Charlie King, and the Calabresis; Jim and Lynn Cameron; Paola and Roland Stearns for their kindness and cooperation; Bill and Joffa Kerr for the privilege of their company in the serene atmosphere of Moose Creek Ranch; Howard Kirschenbaum of Camp Uncas; Kiril Sokoloff for receiving us so graciously at the Adirondack League Club; Craig and Alice Gilborn of the Adirondack Museum; Tom Hill, curator of Thomas County, Georgia, Museum of History; the staff of the Wildlife of the American West Museum, and Steve and Barbara Smith.

Thanks also to our friends in the West who must await another book before we can share our impressions of the remarkable sporting life in those parts: Chopper and Greg Grassell; the indomitable Snook Moore; Bob Wolf, our guide on the Snake River; Jack Dennis, John Bailey, Jan Konigsberg, Tom McGuane, Jonathan Foote, Justin Bridges, Suzanne Schneider of The Sport; Leslie Schwabacher; Dick and Barbara Carlsberg of Brooks Lake Lodge and Debbie Hansen of the Flying A; Bob Coe, Larry Means, Bob Model, Dick Givens, Bill Davis, Ralph Faler, Jerry Fisher, Greg Mentzer, Margery Torrey, and Kelly Wade.

And thanks to friends closer to home: Fayal Greene and her sporting dad, James Barnett; Mary Emmerling, Michelle Wiener, Michael Lane, Mark and Mary Inabit, and George O'Brien; and our intrepid agents, Gayle Benderoff and Deborah Geltman.

We appreciate the efforts of Joan Denman, Howard Klein, Mark McCauslin, Renato Stanisic, and all those at Clarkson Potter who helped us along the way. We also wish to acknowledge the superb design created for this book by our designer Paul Hardy, affable even under pressure, and the sensitive and patient stewardship of the entire project by our editor and friend, Lauren Shakely.

CONTENTS

INTRODUCTION

The scope of America's sporting life is almost unlimited, as varied as the kinds of people and terrain found within its boundaries. The chase and the quarry are the two elements that bind together pursuits as seemingly disparate as fly-fishing and beagling, wing shooting and fox hunting. These are what writer Vance Bourjaily calls the "instinct sports," and he explains that they are "not so much sport as self-renewal . . . and the hunting, which gives shape and purpose to the sojourn, becomes a rite of simplification, in relief of our overconnected domestic and working lives."

America's sporting heritage is a unique set of customs and traditions, and not merely some fainthearted colonial imitation of the hunting, fishing, and shooting pursuits long practiced in Europe. Certain historical factors caused this country's sporting life to develop its own distinctive character. A few of these factors are summarized in the following pages.

REMINDERS OF FAVORITE PURSUITS INFORM MOST HOUSES OF SPORTING FAMILIES, AS IN THE HOME OF ARTIST PETER CORBIN AND HIS WIFE, LILLIAN.

THE NEED TO SHOOT STRAIGHT

As Gary Brumfield, master of the gun shop at Colonial Williamsburg, has pointed out, the reputation and tradition of Americans as gun owners, hunters, and marksmen can be traced to the earliest colonists, who depended on guns for protection as well as hunting for sport and for the table.

THE IZAAK WALTON SCHOLAR DR. RODOLPHE L. COIGNEY HAS COLLECTED 411 OF THE 456 EDITIONS OF *THE COMPLEAT ANGLER.*

Writing about Virginia in 1705, one historian commented, "The people there are very skillful in the use of Fire Arms, being all their Lives accustomed to shoot in the Woods." As our English cousins would find out during the War of Independence, we could shoot in the woods a lot better than they could.

THE EXAMPLE OF NATIVE AMERICANS

Even as they fought the Indians and pushed them off their hunting grounds, early American sportsmen recognized their consummate skills as stalkers, trappers, hunters, and fishers, and learned much from them in the way of materials, techniques, transportation, and woodcraft.

The Indian belief in wild game as a resource free for the taking was a concept radically different from the English and European philosophy, which held that fish and game were the property of the landowners, and poachers beware. White settlers did not consciously adopt the Indian view, but it prevailed in the New World, and the vast amount of public lands and waters

HUMBLE ANGLING MEMENTOS ARE
VALUED AS ICONOGRAPHIC TOKENS
OF TRADITION AND CONTINUITY.

accessible to legal hunting and fishing today in this country is the result. "Wee accounte of them as the Deare in Virginia" is how one early colonist described the status of deer and all wildlife, "things belonging to noe man," and by extension every man.

The deep-seated respect for nature and wildlife of the Native American peoples is at the core of the sporting ethic or code preached by conservation-minded hunters and fishermen of today. This code evolved in the late 19th century as sportsmen like Theodore Roosevelt and Henry Bird Grinnell, longtime editor of *Forest & Stream*, sought to control the reckless depradations of market hunters on rapidly diminishing wildlife populations, most infamously the American bison. In a statement attributed to Chief Seattle upon surrendering the ancestral lands of his Suquamish tribe to the federal government in 1854, the philosophy many sportsmen have come to embrace was expressed: "What is man without the beasts? If all the beasts were gone, man would die from a great loneliness of the spirit. For whatever happens to the beasts, soon happens to man. All things are connected."

THE ROLE OF PRIVATE INITIATIVE

American sporting life strongly bears the imprint of individual, family, and group action, invention, and occasionally, folly. When the railroad penetrated the Adirondacks in the 1870s, sportsmen were soon followed by wealthy industrialists who commissioned "savage meccas for pale pilgrims"—log villas with all the comforts of home, not to mention the bowling alley, and suddenly the wilderness was gentrified.

As early as colonial times, private clubs and land-owning associations were instrumental in adapting English and European hunting and fishing traditions to the unique requirements of American woodlands, waterways, and wildlife.

The Schuylkill Fishing Company, founded in 1732, was only one of numerous clubs that were organized to

THE FORMALITY ASSOCIATED WITH THE FOX HUNT IS EVIDENT IN AN ANTIQUE HUNTSMAN'S
HORN ADORNED WITH A FOXHOUND ALERT FOR THE CHASE.

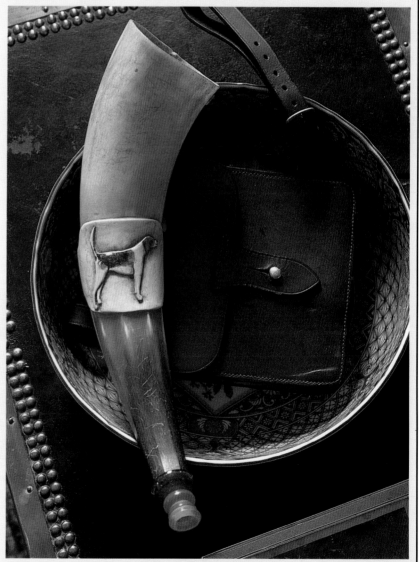

take advantage of the trout waters of south Pennsylvania. The Gloucester Fox Hunt, the first group to ride to hounds on a regular basis, was organized in 1766 in New Jersey. In 1832, the first known gun club was formed by a group of Philadelphians expressly to hunt canvasbacks on Carroll's Island. In 1857, fifteen sportsmen pooled their resources to buy 1,900 acres of marsh and beach property on North Carolina's Outer Banks. Currituck Shooting Club became the first of a number of groups devoted to a new concept in waterfowl gunning. In 1871, the Blooming Grove Park Association formed and established the first game preserve for hunters on 12,000 acres in Pike County, Pennsylvania. The Adirondack League Club, founded in 1890 on nearly 200,000 acres, was one of a number of landowning associations that set a pattern for the controlled development of vast tracts of private lands a century ago.

The wealthy, well-educated membership of many of these clubs may have been elitist, but it was also progressive, managing, not exploiting, the natural and wildlife resources under their control. When the Woodmont Rod and Gun Club was founded in Maryland in 1880, it chose as its motto "Protect and Enjoy," and that typified the enlightened approach of most sporting clubs of the era.

Historian John F. Reiger estimates that by 1890 there were some 300 sporting clubs devoted to field sports, more than 30 angling organizations, numerous gun clubs, and at least a dozen fox-hunting associ-

DOGS ARE CENTRAL TO THE ENJOYMENT AND SUCCESS OF NUMEROUS FIELD SPORTS. ON A POND NEAR HOME, SPORTING ARTIST PETER CORBIN TRAINS HIS RETRIEVER FOR DUCK SEASON.

ations, most of them in the Northeast but with virtually every settled region of the United States represented.

This may well have been the zenith and heyday of this country's sporting experience, for as Wallace Stegner points out, "the distinct downturn in our literature from hope to bitterness took place almost at the precise time when the frontier officially came to an end, in 1890, and when the American way of life had begun to turn strongly urban and industrial."

A BASIC TENET OF SPORTSMEN EVERYWHERE IS TO MAKE USE OF (EAT) ALL FISH AND GAME KILLED.

Today, as many family camps and lodges, gun clubs and other organized hunts struggle just for existence, the conscience of the sporting community resides primarily in conservation groups like Ducks Unlimited, the Boone & Crockett Club, the Atlantic Salmon Foundation, Trout Unlimited, the Audubon Society, and the National Wildlife Federation. Fundraising by such private groups for stewardship pro-

11

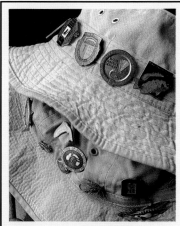

SPORTING FOLK ARE DIEHARD COLLECTORS AND TRAVELERS, *OPPOSITE AND ABOVE.*

grams supplements public monies made available by the Federal Aid in Wildlife Restoration Act of 1937. This act, which levies an 11 percent tax on rifles, shotguns, archery gear, and ammunition, has raised over $2 billion, most of it for state wildlife agencies, with the states adding 25 percent matching funds raised through the sale of fishing and hunting licenses.

THE PATTERN OF REGIONAL EXPRESSION

This underlying component of America's rich sporting heritage has to do with the way individual sporting pursuits have been adapted or changed over time to suit local needs, interests, or whims, or in the case of the southern quail plantation, invented out of the whole cloth of a unique terrain.

The Middleton Hunt in Charleston, South Carolina, for example, is a deer-driven hunt, employing hounds and horses, dating from prior to the Civil War. Originally, hounds were brought to this area to chase the fox, but the thickly wooded country proved unsuitable, so the custom was modified to chase deer instead.

On the Eastern Shore of Maryland, duck hunting is all about artful decoy rigs, and the Winchester Model 12 shotgun is sacrosanct. But in the classic green timber hunts of Arkansas, where hunters stand among the pin oaks in water backed up out of the bayous, there's no respect at all for guns or decoys—a milk carton bobbing in the water is deemed a perfectly adequate decoy. In Arkansas, the cherished centerpiece of the hunt is the duck call, and the hunter's skill in using it to call in migrating mallards.

Regional sporting accents are found as well in architecture, furnishings, boats, and crafts. The neoclassical shooting plantations of the south are the product of the same regional impulse as the rustic wilderness camps and lodges of the Adirondacks. Decoys, trout flies, guideboats, and canoes—all of these sporting elements bear the imprint of local needs, desires, and influences. In terms of aesthetics, our sporting heritage is thoroughly, charmingly decentralized.

REVERENCE FOR THE WILD THING

Americans, and particularly American sportsmen, may care more deeply for nature and wildlife than any other people. Ours is a deeply conflicted passion, however, born of the knowledge that, for a time, we lived in a land of such natural bounty it could have passed for Eden, and yet we passed from it, or, more precisely, permitted the worm of progress to run rampant in the garden.

The first regular column on sports of the field appeared in *American Farmer* in 1825. It was written by

AMONG SPORTSMEN, THE EMOTIONAL (AND FINANCIAL) INVESTMENT IN HANDMADE FIREARMS, FLY RODS, AND OTHER ESSENTIAL TOOLS IS HIGH. HUNTING, FISHING, AND EQUESTRIAN SPORTS ALL HAVE FOSTERED IMPORTANT CRAFTS TRADITIONS.

A SHOOTING TROPHY IN THE HOME OF FOX HUNTERS REMINDS THAT SPORTSMEN HAVE MANY PURSUITS.

John Stuart Skinner, who himself went on to found *American Turf Register* and *Sporting Magazine*. In 1831, the latter periodical began publishing a sporting column that impressed a whole generation of American sportsmen with the English example of the sporting gentleman. It was written by "Frank Forester," the pseudonym of a transplanted British aristocrat named Henry William Herbert. (Ironically, the English upper class of the 19th century is better known for its wretched excesses in the matter of blood sport, as personified in the notorious shooting career of the Earl De Grey. His journals list 370,728 wild animals, from rabbits to rhinos, killed, just for the fun of it, from 1867 to 1900.)

In the 1870s, a spate of new periodicals picked up where Frank Forester left off. *American Sportsman, Forest & Stream, Field & Stream,* and *American Angler* (in 1881) all made their first appearances, and all crusaded for ethical and sportsmanlike behavior in the field, the creation of national parks and refuges, and the end of market hunting (the Lacey Act, passed in 1900, would finally accomplish the last by making illegal the interstate shipment of wildlife or wildlife products).

No other country, in fact, has produced as many elegantly hardheaded, passionate writers on the subject of nature's paradise and its sporting and animal life: Thoreau and Emerson, John Burroughs and John Muir, Theodore Roosevelt (*The Birds of the Adirondacks*, his first book, was published in the late 1870s while he was still at Harvard), the Hemingway who saw through the ambiguities of safaris and two-hearted rivers, and the Robert Ruark who distilled his childhood in rural South Carolina in "The Old Man and the Boy." Then there are Edward Abbey, Edward Hoagland, John McPhee, Peter Mathiessen, Barry Lopez, Annie Dillard, Greta Ehrlich, Jim Harrison, Thomas McGuane, and many others we've overlooked. And for every good writer, there are perhaps a handful of good painters and a dozen good photographers, all enthralled in one way or other with the mystifying beauty and appalling power of the wild and its multitude of creatures, "messengers from another condition of life, another mentality," Hoagland wrote, which "bring us tidings of places where we don't go."

THE COLLECTOR'S RESPECT FOR THE PAST

The couple whose New England farmhouse (page 44) reflects their shared enthusiasm for fine antiques and sporting art began collecting images of the hunt

AT THE CATSKILL FLY FISHING MUSEUM, AN OLD LINE DRYER RECALLS THE ERA OF CASTING WITH LINES MADE OF SILK.

"because we feel these sports are things of the past and that this art is what is left to remind us of them."

Sadly true as their observation may be, America's sporting heritage is preserved in the homes of sporting families and also, today, in a surprisingly large number of superb collections open to the public.

To mention just a few, the American Museum of Fly Fishing in Manchester, Vermont, is a gem of a small museum that even the confirmed bait fisherman would enjoy visiting. The Ward Museum of Wildfowl Art in Salisbury, Maryland, celebrates a century of antique decoys, representing all the major waterfowling areas of the country. Both these museums are planning ambitious expansions, an encouraging sign that our sporting heritage is not being taken for granted.

In the West, both the Wildlife of the American West Art Museum in Jackson, Wyoming, and the Buffalo Bill Historical Center in Cody, Wyoming, have stunning collections of the major 19th-century interpreters of the wilderness experience, from Albert Bierstadt and George Catlin to Winslow Homer and Frederic Remington, as well as many works from the finest contemporary wildlife and sporting artists.

Important ethical, moral, and spiritual values are the basis for the colorful tapestry of *The Sporting Life*. Today, many fishermen practice the policy of "catch and release"—returning unharmed to lake and stream any fish they catch. Many duck hunters voluntarily reduce their limits, or skip hunting season altogether, as drought conditions in breeding grounds continue to reduce duck populations, particularly in the central and Mississippi flyways. Most

SIMPLE ROWBOATS, CUSTOM-MADE GUIDEBOATS, CANOES, PUNT BOATS, AND SNEAK BOATS ALL CARRY THE SPORTSMAN INTO THE WILD—OR JUST ACROSS THE LAKE.

people realize that fox hunts in this country rarely result in a killed fox. No matter what form the chase takes, again and again even its fiercest practitioners will admit that one of the least important goals of the hunt is "bagging a trophy." At the same time, the true sportsman need apologize to no one for taking legal fish or game in fair chase, when he or she makes appropriate use of the catch.

The denizens of *The Sporting Life* are individualists of strong convictions and differing opinions on a vast number of questions, but they tend to share the same vision of the natural world, and man's place in it. But even though they are ardent conservationists, they do not claim to know what the future holds in store for our wild spaces and wildlife. As Aldo Leopold said, "Only the mountain has lived long enough to listen objectively to the howl of the wolf."

This book celebrates the long and pleasant sporting life of North America —and the people who live it.

ANGLING

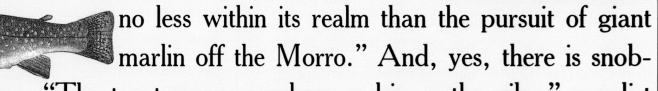

"I am haunted by waters," wrote Norman Maclean in his classic story of fishing the trout rivers of western Montana. All fishermen are haunted by waters, whether plain old farm ponds thick with bass, frozen lakes full of pickerel (if you're hardy enough to jig for them), or the legendary salmon rivers of eastern Canada, where for the average fisherman just to be there falls not far short of a religious experience. "The world of angling is richly diverse," says Nick Lyons, a witty writer and serious publisher in one of his many books about fishing and fishermen. "Carp fishing with dough balls in the Charles River is no less within its realm than the pursuit of giant marlin off the Morro." And, yes, there is snobbism and mystique. "The trout grows nowhere as big as the pike," novelist William Humphrey once observed, "but is there a Pike Unlimited?"

Humphrey's entertaining meditation on angling, *My Moby Dick* (which

TRADITIONS

begins, "Call me Bill."), was inspired by a summer-long quest of a large one-eyed trout in the Berkshires one year. Fishing, especially fly-fishing, is viewed by its most avid practitioners as a form of elemental hunt, requiring knowledge, skill, concentration, and patience. "Even though I wasn't a suicidal child, I grew up wistfully staring off bridges," observes Steve Smith, a maker of trophy fish carvings (see page 208). "I've noticed, or nurtured, the same behavior in my sons. What monster might be under that shadowy ledge in the deepest corner of that pool, and what if I knew he could be mine with one cast? My sons have grown up now, but I never grew out of that fascination."

President Hoover was so enamored of fishing that he wrote a short inspirational volume to convert more young Americans to the hobby, which he touted as a democratizing force: "All men are equal before trout." Jimmy Carter was the keenest fly-fisherman ever to occupy the White House. President Bush, as if determined to fish against type, preferred spin-fishing from a power boat to fly-fishing in waders, the more predictable form of angling for Ivy Leaguers (in fact, Yale, Harvard, and Princeton all have outstanding collections of fly-fishing books and treatises.)

Angling traditions are handed down, like family heirlooms, from one generation to the next. Jim Bowman, who with wife, Judith, collects angling books (see page 64), obtained his first title, *Trout*, by Ray Bergman, from his father when he was sixteen, and "it's still on my desk today," he explains, "for sentimental reasons, and because it is probably the most influential fishing book of the century." On the endpaper it reads, "To Jim from Dad, Xmas 1949—May you continue to go in quest of trout—to far places and as long as you live."

The granddaddy of all fishing books is Izaak Walton's *The Compleat Angler*, first published in England in 1653. Dr. Rodolphe Coigney, in amassing 800 volumes of the work, has pursued Walton with the same passion he has fished for trout and salmon most of his life. "As a practical handbook for modern anglers, it is practically useless," Dr. Coigney observes. A pastoral work extolling the purity and innocence of rural life and celebrating nature, friendship, and good times, *The Compleat Angler* was penned by "a fisherman addicted to worms and grasshoppers, and it was only in the fifth edition that Walton's friend, Charles Cotton, provided a supplement on fly-fishing."

AT THE END OF A DAY OF FISHING, HIGH-TECH FLY RODS AND A VENERABLE WICKER CREEL ARE STOWED ON THE PORCH, A BLEND OF THE OLD AND NEW.

"Going all over the world doesn't make you a top fisherman," pioneering angler and conservationist Lee Wulff let fall during one of his mesmerizing flytying demonstrations a couple of years ago; "it makes you a top traveler." Still, few anglers turn down the chance to test an unfamiliar stream, and most can regale friends with uncannily precise, blow-by-blow descriptions of prize catches from yesterday and from a yesteryear.

About fly-fishing Arnold Gingrich once remarked, "You will meet, if not a better class of people, a better class of fish," and while the pursuit of trout and salmon on a fly does offer the best sport, it is also true that the handcrafts, lore, and traditions associated with those two freshwater game fish are the richest and most diverse in all angling.

"Our whole family loves to eat what we catch," says Jim Bowman in acknowledging yet another custom that many anglers share. "Sautéed trout—ten minutes from the stream. Bass fondue, so good you don't need any sauces other than fresh lemon. Then there's smoked salmon, and Gravad Lax made with fresh dill from a farmer's field up the road from your camp on the Cascapedia."

To join the world of angling is to begin an endless learning process, and some devotees never get enough news of tackle and techniques. As Charles Kuralt, a passionate fisherman himself, wrote, "No pursuit on earth is so burdened by arcane lore as fly-fishing, beside which brain surgery and particle physics are simple backyard pastimes."

Other anglers, convinced there are better ways to measure success, stick to antique fly patterns and familiar pools,

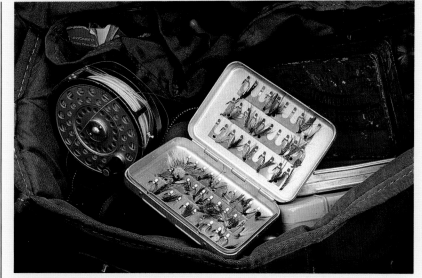

AN ANGLER'S FLY BOX CONTAINS THE PATTERNS MOST LIKELY TO PROVOKE A STRIKE IN THE TROUT WATERS OF THE CATSKILLS, WHERE FLY-FISHING FIRST TOOK HOLD.

and release everything they catch anyway. "Moving through the cool, clear water makes me a part of the river," Joan Wulff said in reflecting on a full fifty years of fishing, "and the act of casting connects me to what I see and feel with a grace and beauty of its own. Through the artificial fly at the end of my leader, I get a glimpse of another world, and can touch another of God's creatures."

Whether romantics or technocrats, anglers are passionate about their fishing places, and they surround themselves with the reminders and emblems of an activity that is part sport, part recreation, and part spiritual retreat. And so, inevitably, collections come into being in the sporting home, and take their humble or elegant shape —gatherings of books, pictures, rods and reels, passels of fly boxes and fish priests and minnow traps, quantities of pure piscatorial whatnot. The rooms fill up. The walls speak the language of fishes. And the angler is well pleased.

AFTER CONSCIENTIOUS ANGLERS HAVE HOOKED THEIR LIMIT, THEY TAKE THEIR CATCH TO THE TABLE.

BIRTHPLACE OF FLY-FISHING

"To celebrate Opening Day on the Beaverkill is a little like observing Christmas in Bethlehem," wrote the columnist and devoted fisherman Red Smith. "For the Beaverkill is the shrine, the fountainhead, the most beloved and best-known trout stream in America. The river of George LaBranche, Theodore Gordon . . . and the Fly Fishers' Club of Brooklyn."

The Fly Fishers' is one of dozens of small, rustic fishing clubs perched along the seven trout streams winding through the Catskill Mountains in New York. These clubs, and similar groups in the Adirondacks, on Long Island, and in Pennsylvania, are historically important because they established fly-fishing customs, codes, and traditions that are pursued to this day.

Of all the clubs, probably none is smaller, or more rustic, than the one founded on farm property in Roscoe, New York, in 1895 by a group of wealthy brewers and zealous fly-fishermen from Brooklyn.

For THESE ARE THE LOTUS EATERS," SPARSE GRAY HACKLE, DEAN OF FISHING WRITERS IN THE 1940S, SAID OF THE FLY FISHERS IN A FAMOUS ESSAY FOR THE *ANGLERS' CLUB BULLETIN.* "THEY LIVE IN A LITTLE WORLD APART, A WORLD WHICH THEY FOUND PERFECT UPON ENTERING AND WHICH, CONSEQUENTLY, THEY STRIVE TO KEEP UNCHANGED." ALTHOUGH LESS THAN 25 PERCENT OF FISHING RIGHTS ON THE CATSKILLS' RIVERS ARE IN PRIVATE HANDS, SOME OF THE BEST POOLS BELONG TO CLUBS LIKE THE FLY FISHERS.

The building itself is and always has been on the verge of total dilapidation and collapse, and that is how the members want it.

The only wealth that matters to the club is its waters, "two and a half miles, both banks, of the sweetest dry-fly water" on the Beaverkill. So long as there are trout in the deep pools of these gin-clear waters, the fly-fishers of Brooklyn won't be seeing electricity and pretty pillows in their clubhouse.

WARNING
Hunting, Fishing Or
Trespassing Forbidden
On This Property

All Persons Found Hunting, Fishing
Or Trespassing On This Property
Will Be Prosecuted According To Law

HOAGY CARMICHAEL, JR., CASTS INTO CLUB WATERS AFTER OBSERVING THE INSECTS CURRENTLY ACTIVE ON THE STREAM. THE BEAVERKILL, A WIDE, GRAVEL-BOTTOM STREAM WITH BOTH NATIVE BROOK TROUT AND THE BROWN TROUT FIRST BROUGHT HERE FROM GERMANY IN THE 1880S, PRODUCES ALL THE MAJOR MAYFLY HATCHES POPULAR WITH DRY-FLY FISHERMEN. LONG STRETCHES OF "NO KILL" WATERS ON THE RIVER ARE OPEN TO FISHING YEAR-ROUND.

A FLYTIER'S COTTAGE

Wherever there is trout or salmon water, there are men and women known for the beauty and effectiveness of their fly patterns—bits of fur, feather, and other exotic or mundane material crafted onto a fishhook.

Poul Jorgensen is a Danish-born mechanical engineer who chucked an unsatisfying corporate career to set up shop at the confluence of two historic streams in Roscoe, New York. "Anyone who can tie his own shoelaces can learn to make flies," Poul modestly observes, and indeed dedicated fly-fishermen insist on making their own patterns—a winter activity that keeps them in touch with their sport. Jorgensen's brightly colored, outsize salmon flies, meant to be enjoyed for their ornamental qualities, not to fish with, fetch high prices with collectors across the country.

JORGENSEN'S BUNGALOW ON THE BANK OF THE WILLOWEMAC IS A BUSY CROSSROADS AND SOCIAL CENTER FOR ANGLERS AND COLLECTORS, A SCENE REPEATED WHEREVER FLYTIERS, THE HIGH PRIESTS AND MEDICINE MEN OF THEIR FISHING COMMUNITIES, HUNCH OVER VISES, IN TACKLE SHOPS AND TROUT TOWNS THROUGHOUT AMERICA.

FLYTYING IS TO ANGLING WHAT DECOY CARVING IS TO DUCK HUNTING. WORKING FLIES, THE EQUIVALENT OF A SHOOTING RIG OF DECOYS, ARE USUALLY DESIGNED TO RESEMBLE LIVE INSECTS OR OTHER CRITTERS ON WHICH FISH FEED. BY THIS MEANS THE WILY HUNTER, WHETHER CHASING FISH OR FOWL, USES ARTIFICE TO MAKE HIS PREY COME TO HIM. JORGENSEN'S DECORATIVE FLIES, TOO EXPENSIVE TO CAST INTO RIVERS, ARE AKIN TO THE WILDFOWLER'S CARVED AND PAINTED BIRDS, DESTINED FOR A FIREPLACE MANTEL OR DESKTOP.

A 22-POUND STEELHEAD TROUT, CAUGHT BY A FRIEND ON THE DEAN RIVER IN BRITISH COLUMBIA, OCCUPIES A PLACE OF HONOR IN JORGENSEN'S LIVING ROOM, *RIGHT,* ALONG WITH *ATLANTIC SALMON FISHING ON THE MATAPEDIA,* A PRINT BY MILTON WHEELER, AND SEVERAL FRAMINGS SHOWING THE FLYTIER'S HANDIWORK. HIS SHELVES ARE FILLED TO THE BRIM WITH REFERENCE BOOKS FOR HIS CRAFT, *LEFT.* IN A CORNER OF THE FLYTIER'S DESK, *BELOW LEFT,* TAILFEATHERS OF PHEASANT AND PEACOCK WAIT TO BE PLUCKED FOR USE IN A FLY PATTERN. JORGENSEN, WHO SPENT SEVEN YEARS LEARNING HIS CRAFT FROM A CHICAGO FLYTIER NAMED BILL BLADES, LIKES TO QUOTE HIS MENTOR. "FLYTYING IS A SCHOOL FROM WHICH WE NEVER GRADUATE."

A TREASURY OF REELS

Somewhere between sculpture and jewelry" is the way Jim Brown, librarian and fly-fisherman, describes the object of his collecting desire, the antique fly reel. "The best examples please the eye, are functional, and speak volumes about the maker's character and technology."

Brown has written two exhaustive monographs on reels, most recently *A Treasury of Reels*, and is permanently on call as house detective on the subject for the American Museum of Fly Fishing in Manchester, Vermont.

As a boy, alongside his grandfather, Brown fished for big bluegills and yellow perch in Lake Champlain, using a cane pole, bobbin, and worm. Today he mainly fly-fishes for trout, releasing almost everything he catches.

"People may fish in different ways, for different species, and for different reasons," he observes, "but we all connect as anglers. The language of fishing cuts across all differences."

JIM BROWN'S ANGLING JOURNAL, THE PLACE MARKED BY A TURN-OF-THE-CENTURY NICKEL SILVER MATCH SAFE FOR KEEPING A FISHERMAN'S MATCHES DRY, REFLECTS THE SAME SCRUPULOUS ATTENTION TO DETAIL THAT MARKS HIS WRITINGS ON FLY REELS. THE NOTATION ON THE WOOD ANEMONE IS SIGNIFICANT TO AN ANGLER BECAUSE ITS APPEARANCE COINCIDES WITH THE HENDRICKSON MAYFLY HATCH, A POWERFUL STIMULUS TO TROUT RISINGS.

EDWARD VOM HOFE, SON OF FREDERICK, MADE HIS PERFECTION TROUT FLY REEL IN ABOUT 1910, "A TIMELESS CLASSIC IN APPEARANCE AND ENGINEERING," SAYS BROWN, STILL BEING COPIED TODAY. THE HARD LEATHER CASE WAS DESIGNED TO PROTECT THE REEL IN TRAVEL AND DURING THE OFF-SEASON. *OUTING*, A MAGAZINE PUBLISHED FROM THE 1880S TO THE 1920S, CATERED TO THE WELL-TO-DO SPORTSMAN WHO WAS LIKELY TO BUY AND USE EQUIPMENT LIKE THE PERFECTION.

FOLLOWING AN AFTERNOON OF INDIVIDUALIZED INSTRUCTION ON THE SPRING-FED STREAM OF FISHING CREEK, FLY-FISHING NOVICES LEAVE THEIR BOOTS AND SOCKS TO DRY AND SEEK OUT FRIENDS TO REGALE WITH THEIR FIRST "THE ONE THAT GOT AWAY" STORIES.

FISHING SCHOOL

Cathy and Barry Beck, outfitters on Fishing Creek in rural Benton, Pennsylvania, run one of the many fly-fishing schools now proliferating in America's trout country. The instruction ranges from classroom basics on fly rods, reels, and lines; casting lessons on the lawn ("10 o'clock to 2 o'clock, 10 o'clock to 2 o'clock . . ."); to, finally, a half day on the river itself, in waders and with the necessary gear to cast dry flies, nymphs, and streamers. Students even get a chance to catch a fat trout (on a stocked pond), bring it to net, properly remove the hook, and release it back into the water.

CATHY BECK BRIEFS STUDENTS ON THE IMPORTANCE OF UNDERSTANDING STREAM ECOLOGY IN PURSUING TROUT IN ALL SEASONS. IN RECENT YEARS EQUAL NUMBERS OF WOMEN AND MEN HAVE TAKEN UP FLY-FISHING AS A RELAXING BUT CHALLENGING SPORT. CAREFUL HANDLING IN BRINGING A TROUT TO NET, *RIGHT*, AND REMOVING THE HOOK FROM ITS MOUTH HELP TO ENSURE THE FISH'S SURVIVAL.

A STAFF MEMBER TIES A FLY TO A PUPIL'S LEADER, DRAWING ON VEST POCKETS CHOCK-FULL OF THE TOOLS AND EQUIPMENT NEEDED TO MAKE ON-STREAM ADJUSTMENTS IN ANGLING STRATEGY, FROM SCISSORS, PLIERS, AND SPOOLS OF THREAD TO A COLLAPSIBLE BUTTERFLY NET FOR SNAGGING INSECTS, AND EVEN A MINIATURE STOMACH PUMP, FOR EXAMINING FOOD THE FISH ARE FEEDING ON THAT DAY.

ALLURES OF ANGLING

They call him "New-in-the-Box" Beck because he passionately collects old bait-and-tackle shop products in their original packaging, but, like many accumulators of angling ephemera, John Beck of Houston, Texas, "can't quite explain why it grabs and holds me." It's like taking his grandson fishing, "just something I have to do and love to do."

Perhaps it is the colorful graphics and hard-sell promises ("Catch More Fish!") that make so engaging yesterday's advertising material, product packaging, and special-interest magazines aimed at fishermen. They represent a commercial art form as emblematic of our way of life, and our crazy-quilt economy, as breakfast cereal and bubble gum cards.

ABOVE LEFT, MINNOWS ARE AMONG THE OLDEST SPORTFISHING LURES EVER MADE AND A FAVORITE OF BASS FISHERMEN. *FAR LEFT,* AN OLD GLASS MINNOW TRAP FROM SHAKESPEARE, FORMERLY THE KALAMAZOO FISHING TACKLE COMPANY, IS FILLED WITH BRIGHTLY PAINTED FISHING FLOATS. *LEFT,* BOTH THE LEATHER TACKLE BOX AND THE BOX'S CONTENTS ARE COLLECTIBLES. *OPPOSITE,* JOHN BECK'S OLD BUGS, MINNOWS, AND OTHER BAITS, MOST OF THEM MADE IN THE 1920S AND 1930S, APPEAR TO HAVE TUMBLED FROM SOME DUSTY TACKLE BOX IN GREAT-GRANDDAD'S ATTIC. "VENABLE'S CHARMER," A MINNOW MADE OF CORK AND FEATHERS, WAS ONE IN A SERIES OF WILDER-DILG LURES THAT TRADED ON CELEBRITY SPORTSMEN. "FISH AND FEEL FIT" WAS A WARTIME SLOGAN TO COUNTER THE BELIEF THAT FISHING WAS ONLY FOR KIDS, IDLERS, OR NE'ER-DO-WELLS.

UNTIL RECENTLY, OLD TACKLE CATALOGS, *OPPOSITE,* WERE LIGHTLY REGARDED BY ANTIQUARIANS, BUT NOW THEY ARE COLLECTOR'S ITEMS IN THEIR OWN RIGHT, BOTH FOR THEIR HISTORIC INFORMATION AND GRAPHIC APPEAL. "LURES WITH FISH APPEAL" OF THE HEISER COMPANY, *RIGHT,* SUCH AS THE ALBINO GHOST, YELLOW LOON, AND CHINESE FURY HAD BRIGHTLY PAINTED CORK BODIES EMBELLISHED WITH FEATHERS AND DEER HAIR.

THE ANGLERS' CLUB

Piscatoribus Sacrum" reads the sign over the entrance to the Anglers' Club of New York, a fisherman's retreat in the canyons of Wall Street, and sacred indeed is the atmosphere of its book-filled rooms, graced with sporting pictures by Ogden Pleissner and a fireplace mantel from the historic Fraunces Tavern.

Presidents Harding, Coolidge, Hoover, and Eisenhower all were members of the club, which was started as a "fly and casting club" by eleven zealous anglers in a borrowed meeting room at the offices of *Field & Stream* in 1905. That early literary connection presaged a long involvement, continuing to this day, by the club and club members in the reporting and interpreting of the angling experience. Some fifty club members have authored close to 200 different books on fishing. The club's *Bulletin* has offered a blend of notes from the rivers of the world, personal essays, and scholarship since 1920. And its 1,500 volumes have been justly described as "one of the finest libraries of angling literature in the world."

TIMEWORN PEWTER TROPHIES, *LEFT,* ATTESTING TO A BYGONE ERA WHEN CASTING TOURNAMENTS PROMOTED SKILLS WITH THE FLY ROD, ARE RANGED AGAINST BOUND VOLUMES OF THE CLUB'S ONGOING CONTRIBUTION TO ANGLING LITERATURE. THE INTIMATE READING ROOM, *BELOW,* LENDS ITSELF TO STUDY AND REFLECTION; IN ADDITION TO BOOKS, THE CLUB MAINTAINS A COLLECTION OF CANE RODS, HISTORIC AUTOGRAPHS, 19TH-CENTURY PHOTOGRAPHS, AND AN ASSORTMENT OF DRY FLIES.

THE ANGLERS' CLUB WELCOMES MEMBERS WITH AN OLD-FASHIONED SIGN, *LEFT.* THE FIREPLACE, *RIGHT,* SURMOUNTED BY A 32-POUND ATLANTIC SALMON CAUGHT BY HELEN C. BARBOUR IN 1934, ALSO DISPLAYS A PAIR OF SILVER CHALICES WON BY EDWARD R. HEWITT FOR LONG-DISTANCE FLY CASTING AT THE WORLD'S FAIR IN CHICAGO IN 1904, AND FLY-FISHING PIONEER THEODORE GORDON'S DRY FLIES. *BELOW,* A COMPLETE SET OF FLY PATTERNS ASSEMBLED IN 1887 BY FREDERIC M. HALFORD, THE ENGLISHMAN WHO BROUGHT DRY FLIES TO AMERICA, HANGS IN PERMANENT TRIBUTE TO ANOTHER OF THE LEGENDARY INNOVATORS OF ANGLING. THE FOOT-LONG SILVER PRIEST IS A CEREMONIAL VERSION OF THE BLUNT WEAPON TRADITIONALLY USED TO KILL FISH WHEN LANDED.

PERSONALIZED TABLE SETTINGS, *LEFT,* LEND A FORMAL NOTE TO THE LONG TABLE WHERE MEMBERS PARTAKE OF LUNCH, THEN DIG INTO "ANGLERS' CLUB CAVIAR"—FISHING STORIES. THE FLYTIER'S DESK, *ABOVE,* A SERENE COMPANION TO A WALL OF ANGLING TITLES, WAS MADE BY ROBERT S. KINSEY, A MEMBER, AND IS CALLED INTO SERVICE WHEN VISITING TIERS DEMONSTRATE THEIR ART ON "CRACKERBARREL NIGHT."

THEODORE GORDON'S HISTORIC ROLE IN AMERICAN ANGLING ACCOUNTS FOR THE STATUS OF "HOLY RELIC" ACCORDED HIS ALUMINUM FLY BOX. IN 1890, AFTER RECEIVING FOUR DOZEN ENGLISH DRY FLIES FROM FREDERIC M. HALFORD, GORDON REALIZED THAT THESE IMPORTED LURES WERE UNSUITABLE FOR U.S. WATERS AND PROCEEDED TO DESIGN HIS OWN PATTERNS BASED ON NATIVE INSECTS. HIS WRITINGS IN *FOREST & STREAM* AND FREQUENT LECTURES HELPED TO LAUNCH THE BOOM IN FLY-FISHING IN THE EARLY YEARS OF THE CENTURY. THE SILVER FLY FISHERS' CLUB LIGHTER IN THE FORM OF A LEAPING SALMON ORIGINALLY WAS AN ORNAMENT FOR THE RADIATOR CAP ON AN ENGLISH MOTOR CAR.

THEODORE GORDON'S FLY BOX
Presented by William Naden
1955

ATOP A PRIZED COLLECTION OF EARLY FLY REELS, THE OUTING CHAMPIONSHIP CUP AND A PUNCH BOWL CALLED THE HOME POOL SERVE AS REMINDERS OF THE CLUB'S HISTORIC TRADITIONS, AND SENSE OF HUMOR.

BATTENKILL FARMHOUSE

The Battenkill River rises in the Green Mountains, flows through the picture-perfect postcard of southern Vermont, and then makes an abrupt westward turn into New York, emptying, finally, in the Hudson River. All along it are found anglers in season.

The Battenkill is one of the most famous trout streams in America, known particularly for its elusive grandfather brown trout, some weighing five pounds or more, lurking in the riffles and holding pools.

Not surprising, then, that a sporting family who fish, hunt, and shoot all over the world always make it a point to return to their farmhouse on the Battenkill in the month of May. For that is when the Hendrickson hatch occurs on the stream, an insect so

44

AN 1840 FARMHOUSE THAT WAS IN THE SAME FAMILY FOR NEARLY 150 YEARS IS NOW THE DOMAIN OF A BUSY HOUSEHOLD OF ANGLERS, SHOOTERS, AND HUNTERS. WITH ITS HAND-FLUTED PILLARS AND LOG CONSTRUCTION, THE HOUSE, ORIGINALLY BUILT AS A WEDDING PRESENT, REFLECTS THE STURDY VALUES OF YANKEE CRAFTSMANSHIP. THE FAMILY OF TRANSPLANTED MIDWESTERNERS, WITH THEIR COMMITMENT TO WILDLIFE CONSERVATION AND ETHICAL CONDUCT IN FIELD AND STREAM, BRING TO THIS ABODE SPORTING STANDARDS JUST AS DURABLE AND HARD-WON—AS SOLID AS A CAST-IRON DOORSTOP IN THE IMAGE OF A PHEASANT, *OPPOSITE BOTTOM.*

appetizing to the trout that it stimulates uncommonly lively strikes.

"It can be the best of the year's fly-fishing," says the man of the house. "Turkey season also opens in early May, so I have the best of both worlds—calling in gobblers between 4:00 and 4:30 A.M., and sneaking away from the office to fish between 2:00 and 3:00 P.M., when the Hendrickson flies hatch."

His wife, a keen fly-fisher and cookbook author, usually loves to cook what is caught using the savory wild fish and game recipes she has collected and refined, or created outright, over the years. But in the case of the Battenkill's precious trout, she prefers to release her fish and replace it with store-bought sole in her recipes.

Interest in wild tastes started early in this sporting family, and on both sides.

VOLUMES ON ICHTHYOLOGY, *ABOVE,* SUGGEST THAT SOMETHING IS FISHY IN THIS SPORTING FAMILY, BUT LIKE MANY CLANS RAISED IN THE TRADITIONS OF THE CHASE, THE HOUSEHOLD CONDUCTS PURSUIT IN ALL DIRECTIONS. THE LIVING ROOM, *LEFT,* CELEBRATES A FASCINATION WITH WATERFOWL, WHILE THE DEN, *RIGHT,* IS A MIXTURE OF SPORTING IMAGES, INCLUDING *LYE BROOK POOL,* BY OGDEN PLEISSNER, AND A ROYAL STAG TAKEN BY THE OWNER IN SCOTLAND. THE OLD SHOTGUNS WERE BROUGHT BACK FROM THE CIVIL WAR BY A VERMONT SOLDIER.

THE LAD IN THE PICTURE WAS TWO YEARS OLD WHEN HIS INTREPID MOTHER (PREGNANT AT THE TIME) SET FORTH TO BAG A FEW ALLIGATORS ON LAKE MICCOSUKEE IN NORTHERN FLORIDA. "A PUNTER POLED HER AROUND IN THE SWAMP IN A SKIFF UNTIL SHE SAW A GATOR, USUALLY SHOOTING IT IN THE EYE FROM 70 TO 100 YARDS," HE RECALLS.

WALTER, AN ENGLISH SETTER, CHECKS OUT THE RUFFED GROUSE BROUGHT BACK FROM THE FIELD THAT MORNING. DESTINED FOR THE DINNER TABLE, ANIMALS CAUGHT AS GAME TEND TO RECEIVE MUCH MORE RESPECTFUL TREATMENT THAN THE AVERAGE STORE-BOUGHT CHICKEN OR BEEF. "THINK ABOUT IT," SAYS THE SPORTSWOMAN WHO LIVES HERE. "THE AVERAGE LIFE SPAN OF A GAME BIRD LIKE A QUAIL IS 15 TO 18 MONTHS. I PERSONALLY WOULD RATHER EAT ONE THAN LET A SKUNK, COON, FOX, OR HAWK GET IT. NATURE TAKES HUNDREDS MORE THAN WE MANAGE TO SHOOT."

"I remember eating a quail my dad had shot in Ohio when I was four years old," she recalls. "It was considered so special I have never forgotten how delicious it was."

Her husband's first quail of childhood made a different impression. "When I was four or five, we were in Georgia and my folks loaded me in the shooting buggy and took me out on a quail hunt," he recalls. "I didn't like them killing the birds, so every time they missed a shot, I'd say, 'Bad for you, but good for me.' At one point I even replaced the shot in their cartridges with sand!"

FISH AND GAME COOKERY'S IMPORTANCE TO THE BATTENKILL FARMHOUSE MAY BE SEEN IN THE CUSTOM KITCHEN, COMPLETE WITH AN OUTSIZED 1903 JEWETT REFRIGERATOR, COMMERCIAL RANGE, DUCK PRESS, PLENTY OF SPACE FOR COOKBOOKS, AND SHALLOW SHELVES FOR STORING TERRINES AND VESSELS WITH SPORTING MOTIFS. THE CARVED SALMON IS AN OLD FISHMONGER'S SIGN BROUGHT BACK FROM ENGLAND.

AN ARTIST'S FISHING ROOM

Christopher Cook describes his exhibit as "part country tackle shop, part church," with thousands of angling objects, from hand-painted floats and lures to family mementos from three generations. An artist in Andover, Massachusetts, Cook is a lifelong angler with five different fishing boats parked in his front yard. He collected most of his old tackle at flea markets and garage sales during the 1950s, and made, carved, or painted a number of the other ingredients in the compelling spectacle.

Nothing is labeled in the Fishing Room, yet as one observer noted, it is "a combination of history, ethnography, natural science, and art in a form that is immediately accessible and deeply rewarding."

AN ALLIGATORED DOOR, *LEFT,* WELCOMED VISITORS TO COOK'S "ENVIRONMENTAL INSTALLATION" WHEN IT WAS MOUNTED AT THE ADDISON GALLERY OF AMERICAN ART IN ANDOVER. EIGHT YEARS IN THE MAKING, THE EXHIBIT PROVOKED A VARIETY OF WONDROUS REACTIONS. ONE YOUNG WOMAN FOUND IT "ALMOST TERRIFYING, THE PURE WEAPONRY OF IT." A LOCAL FISHERMAN CAME BY AND SAT IN THE ROOM FOR FOUR HOURS, DUMBFOUNDED, NEVER SAYING A WORD.

In what Cook calls his most surreal composition, the case atop the display of early tackle-shop products combines disparate elements such as a toy submarine and a jumping jack from the artist's childhood, and a peevish letter from angling pioneer Charles Orvis to an underachieving heating contractor. The fish on top of the case, hand carved and painted by the artist, is "a cross between a bonefish and a salmonid."

AS A TRIBUTE TO THE GEOMETRIC FORMS HE SEES BROUGHT INTO THE ARTIFACTS OF ANGLING BY THE HUMAN HAND, COOK ARRANGED THIS STILL LIFE OF FLOAT, BOBBER, AND IRON CONE (THE PROTECTIVE TIP FROM A CANOE POLE USED ON THE MATAPEDIA RIVER IN CANADA) INSIDE A DISPENSER CASE FROM AN OLD-FASHIONED CANDY STORE. AS ONE CRITIC POINTED OUT, THE FISHING ROOM IS "THE ACCUMULATED PARAPHERNALIA OF AN OBSESSIVE PASSION."

THIS ARRAY OF PRE-1940 BASS LURES, "MADE TO CATCH FISHERMEN AS MUCH AS TO CATCH FISH," NOTES COOK, IS JUXTAPOSED WITH OLD POSTCARDS BOASTING OF APOCRYPHAL CATCHES ON LAKE AND STREAM. IN DESCRIBING THE EXHIBIT, GALLERY DIRECTOR JOCK REYNOLDS WROTE, "THE SEDUCTIVENESS, BEAUTY, AND TRICKERY EMBODIED IN A LURE REMIND US HOW MAN HAS ALWAYS SOUGHT TO IMITATE AND TRANSFORM THE WONDER OF NATURE FOR PRACTICAL AND AESTHETIC PURPOSES."

AN OLD GUN CASE HOUSES LURES ARRANGED BY THE ARTIST'S DAUGHTER, ESTHER, TO RESEMBLE "FISHES SWIMMING UP AND DOWN"; SOME OF THE LURES WERE CARVED AND PAINTED BY COOK. OVER THE CASE IS A PRINTED AND EMBOSSED FISH, ONE IN A SERIES DISTRIBUTED TO BAIT AND TACKLE SHOPS BY THE WEBER LIFELIKE FLY COMPANY A HALF CENTURY AGO.

A NATURAL HISTORY

I'm convinced it's in the genes," David Kettlewell says to explain the aptitude for natural history that runs in his family, accenting every room in the 1769 colonial brick farmhouse he shares with his wife, Miranda, children Alice and Henry, a black Lab, a Jack Russell, a cage full of gerbils, a snake, and a few birds.

The Kettlewells, both British, have been living and working in Connecticut for the past twelve years, and their house is a comfortable mix of English elegance and Yankee rusticity. They both come from sporting families: Miranda fished the chalk streams of Berkshire as a girl and lived eleven years in Kenya; and David grew up in South Africa and thereafter in

IN THE DRAWING ROOM, *LEFT*, IMAGES OF MIRANDA'S FOREBEARS, MOST NOTABLY REVEREND RICHARD NEWCOMBE, A RECTOR IN 17TH-CENTURY SUFFOLK, ARE GATHERED ON THE MANTEL, WHILE DAVID'S FATHER, DR. BERNARD KETTLEWELL, IS REMEMBERED ON THE FAMILY-ALBUM TABLE, IMMORTALIZED IN A 1958 *HOLIDAY* ARTICLE BY HUMORIST LUDWIG BEMELMANS AS "THE BEST TYPE OF ENGLISHMAN, HEARTY AND JOVIAL . . . AT HIS LIGHT-TRAP, VEILED BY A KITE-NET, STRIPPED TO THE WAIST, AND COVERED WITH MOTHS." *ABOVE*, HENRY CARRIES ON THE FAMILY SPORTING TRADITION.

England, where he enjoyed hunting pheasant and partridge and, most years, making trips to Scotland in pursuit of salmon.

The impulse to collect can be traced directly to David's father, Dr. Bernard Kettlewell, the first naturalist to demonstrate that Darwin's theory of natural selection really happens, in his seminal work, *The Evolution of Melanism*. Thousands of the moths he collected as research are now on exhibit as part of the British Museum's Rothschild-Cockayne-Kettlewell Collection.

There seems little doubt that the next generation will carry on the fishing/hunting instinct and conservation ethic as well. "Henry was just three when we put him next to a stream with a stick with a string on it," Miranda notes, "and he sat there, happily, for hours."

THE WILLIAM AND MARY WALNUT SECRETARY, *LEFT,* A PRIZED FAMILY HEIRLOOM, STORES RARE FIRST EDITIONS AND REFERENCE WORKS OF THE NATURAL SCIENCES, WHILE AN ANTIQUE IVORY-HANDLED SPECIMEN CASE, *RIGHT,* REVEALS THE PENCHANT FOR CLASSIFYING NATURAL PHENOMENA THAT WAS A HALLMARK OF BRITISH SCIENCE, AND THE BURGEONING SCHOOL OF FLY-FISHING, IN THE 19TH CENTURY.

THE OLDEST ROOM IN THE KETTLEWELL HOUSE, *ABOVE,* SERVES AS FAMILY ROOM AND THE REPOSITORY FOR THE SPECIMENS OF NATURE BROUGHT BACK FROM SURROUNDING GARDENS AND WOODS. A LUNA MOTH AND OTHER INSECTS, FIXED ON SETTING BOARDS WITH PINS, *LEFT,* SHARE SPACE WITH A CURLEW CARVED OUT OF DRIFTWOOD BY GEORGE BARNES, AND DR. KETTLEWELL'S MICROSCOPE FROM MEDICAL SCHOOL DAYS. A DOWNSTAIRS BATHROOM, *RIGHT,* HAS BEEN TAKEN OVER BY FISHING GEAR.

THE UNCAGED WOMAN

More books have been written in the English language on fishing than just about any other subject, so it's no surprise that wonderful angling libraries often grace the homes, retreats, and other sanctuaries of sporting families.

"Most fly-fishermen have a touch of the poet in them," observes Judith Bowman. The 1876 colonial she and her husband, Jim, occupy in Bedford, New York, overflows with the couple's personal book collection as well as a host of fishing titles for Judith's rare-book business, called The Uncaged Woman.

It was Jim, a recently retired publisher, who provided the name twenty years ago from *Familiar Fish* by Eugene McCarthy (1900): "Every healthy boy, every right-minded man, and every uncaged woman, feels at one time or another, and maybe at all times, the impulse to go 'a fishing."

The name caught on so well that "now my office walls are covered with antique postcards of fishing ladies from all over the world," says Judith.

TITLES FROM THE GILDED AGE OF BOOKBINDING, *RIGHT*, INCLUDE *FISHING AND FLY-MAKING*, BY JOHN HARRINGTON KEENE (1887) AND *A QUAINT TREATISE*, BY W. H. ALDAM (1876). TOPPING THE LOT IS A UNIQUE AUTHOR'S COPY OF *FISHERMEN'S PHILOSOPHY*, BY GEORGE A. ZABRISKIE (1935), WITH A SNAKESKIN COVER SIMULATING FISH SCALES. FLYTIER CHARLES KROM CREATED A SALMON FLY, *BELOW*, FOR JUDITH BOWMAN; APPROPRIATELY, IT IS KEPT HARD BY *THE RESTIGOUCHE AND ITS SALMON FISHING*, BY DEAN SAGE, PUBLISHED IN EDINBURGH IN 1888 IN AN EDITION OF 100 COPIES.

"THE TYPICAL ANGLING BOOK COLLECTOR IS KEENLY INTERESTED IN THE HISTORY OF THE SPORT, THE REMINISCENCES OF FISHERMEN FROM ANOTHER ERA, AND ACCOUNTS OF FISHING STREAMS AND CATCHING FISH THAT MOST OF US CAN ONLY DREAM ABOUT," SAYS BOWMAN. WITH A PENSIVE IZAAK WALTON LOOKING ON, THE BOOK DEALER'S DESK IS CROSSED BY HUNDREDS OF ANGLING ANTIQUITIES.

THE BOWMANS PLAN ONE UNUSUAL FLY-FISHING TRIP EACH YEAR SOMEWHERE OUTSIDE OF NORTH AMERICA, RETURNING WITH LOCAL INSIGNIA, *LEFT*, INDIGENOUS FLY PATTERNS, AND MEMORIES. *BELOW*, A RARE 1814 VOLUME DEVOTED TO THE "PLEASING AND NATIONAL RECREATION" OF ANGLING HAS THE BONUS SUPPLEMENT, "NOBB'S COMPLETE TROLLER."

ON THE WING

"I have a rival in every bird," Lucy Audubon once said, remarking on the obsessive interest of her husband, the French émigré painter John James Audubon, in the avian population of the New World. We know the result of that obsession: *Birds of America*, the magnificent engravings, published a few at a time from 1827 to 1838, of Audubon's unique watercolor portraits of virtually all of our native bird species, "a kind of museum of a wilderness that was already becoming remote," according to one critic, who went on to praise the naturalist master as "the nearest thing American art has had to a founding father."

Suffice it to say that the families and friends of devoted wing shooters in

America "have a rival" in every game bird that exists. But it is not just the wildfowl that accounts for the addictive nature of their chosen pursuit. In habits and natural habitats, duck and geese, impish woodcock in their upland coverts, the ruffed grouse (partridge) of the East, and the

A TEXAS BANQUET OF GRILLED DOVE AND QUAIL MARKS THE END OF A REWARDING DAY OF SHOOTING.

sage grouse of the West, the rail, snipe, pheasant, and quail distinctly differ, providing a rich and complex range of experiences to the pursuer. Grouse run away through the underbrush at a hunter's approach, for example, taking to wing unpredictably if at all, while quail rise in startled coveys and fly with *commitment*.

Naturally, such differences among species are fascinating to the hunter of birds and sometimes of no small tactical interest.

Most hunters have a favorite quarry. For gun engraver Winston Churchill (see page 124), it is the ruffed grouse of his native Vermont. "The explosive flush of grouse is music to my ears," he says. "I long for it, anticipate it, and prepare for it, but it's always a surprise, and I never quite get used to it, no matter how many times I hear it."

Dr. Rodolphe Coigney has collected hundreds of books devoted to the woodcock. "I have a real passion for that bird," he admits. "It is the most mysterious, enigmatic, whimsical, disconcerting, and yet most intelligent of birds. The way it reacts to man or dog is always unexpected or unforeseeable."

Apart from the variety in the prey there is the firearm itself, and all the training, skill building, and care associated with it, whether it be a standard over-and-under shotgun or a hand-tooled heirloom handed down from grandfather's time—or freshly engraved, at considerable expense, by an accomplished craftsman like Winston Churchill.

"My typical client is an art lover first and an arms collector second," Churchill observes, "so the firearm I engrave for him will probably never be shot—he has others to use in the field." He believes hunting provides "an oasis of truth in lives that have become distant, highly technical, and artificial." The emotional appeal in a weapon never to be fired lies in its engraving, he says, "the attempt to bring home in a permanent way the fleeting beauty of the hunt, the wildlife, and the natural habitat."

A GROUPING OF CONTEMPORARY DECOYS EXHIBITS SOME OF THE BEST WORK OF A HISTORIC STRATFORD, CONNECTICUT, CARVING TRADITION.

Important customs are handed down along with favorite guns. Artist Peter Corbin was raised in a house full of Labrador retrievers, fly rods, shotguns, and the collected "shooting pictures" of A. B. Frost. "My father presented me with my first shotgun at the age of six," Corbin recalls. "It was a light 410 gauge with exposed hammers. I hunted pheasants with my older brother and father at game preserves for three and a half years with an empty gun. It was a wonderful way to learn safety."

BRITAIN'S SHOOTING SPORTS START WITH FINELY TOOLED GUNS, GUN CASES, AND CARTRIDGE POUCHES.

Finally, dogs almost always play a crucial and cherished role in wing shooting, as pointers or retrievers, or both, and as companions in the wild world. The breeding and training and sheer time, thought, and devotion that go into the making of a good gundog are enormous, and few sporting families can stand to be without at least a couple.

Each form of wing shooting elicits its own demands and protocol, just as each successful hunt brings out a favorite family recipe. The family of "Masters of the Chase" (see page 127), for example, always serve ruffed grouse for dinner on Christmas Eve, with a currant and juniper berry sauce, wild rice, and ratatouille made from vegetables grown in the garden. "It's the responsibility of each family member to get his or her grouse," reports the mother of the clan, "and in the lean grouse years it is not beyond one's pride to gather up a fresh road-kill!"

The sporting life is a study in contrasts. The genteel rituals of the southern quail plantation, unlike most forms of hunting, take place in reasonably decent weather and during bankers' hours. For something completely different, try the rigors of sea-duck hunting from a small layout boat on a heaving winter sea off the coast of Maine, at dawn.

But all good sport is hard won, and sometimes lost. More duck-hunting clubs have closed their doors in recent years than not, yet many of those that remain have worked mightily to preserve the marsh and wetland habitat essential for waterfowl survival. Nature lovers also benefit from the hunters' zeal.

The resource-management job of quail plantation owners is neverending, involving annual burnings over vast areas as well as special plantings of feed patches, harrowing, mowing, and selective timber cuts. The burnings are necessary to keep the land in an open pine woodland state and prevent the rise of a dense hardwood thicket, which would doom quail and many other species that thrive there now.

Only people who really care about the quality of their chosen sporting life will go to this much trouble to preserve it. Audubon was a relentless shooter of birds as well as an artist, but he could not have foreseen the slaughter of wildlife by commercial hunters. As he lay dying, roused by the arrival of an old friend, he reportedly called out, "Yes, yes, Billy! You go down that side of Long Pond, and I'll go this side, and we'll get the ducks."

IN THE HEART OF QUAIL-PLANTATION COUNTRY, A FAVORITE QUARRY OCCUPIES A PLACE OF HONOR.

A HISTORIC SHOOTING CLUB

Winous Point Shooting Club, overlooking 4,500 acres of pristine marsh and wetlands on Sandusky Bay, Ohio, is believed to be the oldest duck-hunting club operating under continuous charter in America, with several families who belong today tracing memberships since before the Civil War.

The club has been managed by wildlife biologists since 1946, decades before most people became aware of the need for professional supervision of natural habitats. A model sportsmen's organization, Winous Point has generated, through sponsorship of doctorate and master's research projects on the premises, critical findings about wetlands, waterfowl,

THE WILD RICE, WILD CELERY, AND OTHER AQUATIC PLANTS GROWING IN THE SHALLOW MARSHES AT THE WESTERN END OF SANDUSKY BAY, *OPPOSITE,* PROVIDE AN IMPORTANT FOOD RESOURCE FOR MIGRATING WATERFOWL EVERY FALL. A CANADA GOOSE WEATHER VANE ON TOP OF THE CLUBHOUSE, *RIGHT AND ABOVE,* IS CONNECTED BY A 30-FOOT SHAFT TO A WIND-DIRECTION INDICATOR INSIDE THE ROOM WHERE MEMBERS DRAW LOTS FOR DUCK BLIND SELECTION BEFORE A DAY OF HUNTING.

and other wildlife that are helping to guide the restoration of marshes not just in Ohio but elsewhere in North America, too.

In setting aside its 2,400-acre Muddy Creek Bay as a refuge area for migrating waterfowl, it has provided a biologically important stopover for such hard-pressed species as the black duck. At the peak of the fall migration, more than 100,000 ducks have been counted here, and as many as 40,000 black ducks, half the number that travel the entire Mississippi flyway.

Winous Point is steeped in heritage, tradition, and character. Its 125 years of shooting records are being put on the computer now, but the old, tried-and-true customs of the hunt still prevail. One unwritten rule obtains: "Don't talk shop on the marsh." Over the years, duck clubs have sold out to mobile-home parks, condo developments, and marinas, but the members here, recognizing the marshes are an integral part of their cherished family traditions, have elected to sustain the valuable wetlands in perpetuity.

RIGS OF DECOYS, STOWED IN MEMBERS' LOCKERS WHEN NOT IN USE, *ABOVE,* ARE SET OUT ON THE MARSH FROM CENTURY-OLD PUNT BOATS, *BELOW,* POLED THROUGH THE SHALLOWS BY GUIDES CALLED PUNTERS. EVERY SUMMER, 5-BY-16-FOOT MATS ARE FASHIONED AS PORTABLE BLINDS FROM NATIVE BLUE JOINT GRASS, *RIGHT.* ARTICULATED OARS MAKE IT POSSIBLE FOR A PERSON TO SIT LOOKING IN THE DIRECTION HE IS ROWING.

HIGH-FLYING IMAGES

As any visitor to Donal O'Brien's Connecticut home is likely to surmise, birds mean a lot to him. They come in a host of forms—carvings, paintings, walking sticks, and the Audubon prints that remind the owner of his productive and gratifying tenure as chairman of the National Audubon Society.

Duck decoys, which lend their serene, understated presence to many of the rooms in the 1790 house, have played an integral part in Donal's life since boyhood. "I would cut them out of my grandfather's shooting rig," he recalls, "and then take them into my bedroom—they were my toy trucks and teddy bears." Since then he has become an accomplished carver of decoys and birds, and a passionate collector, spending his initial years searching out decoys at their source rather than trafficking in them at galleries or auctions.

Donal, wife Katie, and their four children devoted almost all their vacations as a young family to fishing, hunting, and bird-watching excursions. "It taught our children both self-reliance and teamwork," he says, "and values—it gave them an environmental ethic as it exposed them to the wonders of nature."

A 1790 COLONIAL HOUSE, *OPPOSITE,* ORIGINALLY OCCUPIED BY THE TOWN MILLER, NOW CONTAINS THE HANDIWORK OF ARTISTS AND CRAFTSMEN WORKING IN TIME-HONORED SPORTING TRADITIONS. THE WEATHERVANE, *RIGHT,* WAS CRAFTED BY BLACKSMITH WARREN GILKER, SUPERINTENDENT OF DONAL O'BRIEN'S FAVORITE SALMON LODGE. THE BACKYARD STREAM, *BELOW,* IS A HAVEN FOR THE WILDLIFE HELD IN SUCH HIGH ESTEEM BY THE FAMILY.

*O*CTOBER *MORNING,* BY OGDEN PLEISSNER, WAS COMMISSIONED BY DONAL O'BRIEN AND DEPICTS HIS SON AND DOG, BLUE, RUFFED GROUSE HUNTING IN THE NORTHEAST KINGDOM OF VERMONT. PLEISSNER, ONE OF AMERICA'S MOST NOTABLE SPORTING ARTISTS, WAS A FAMILY FRIEND AND THIS INTIMATE SITTING ROOM CONTAINS SEVERAL EXAMPLES OF HIS EXQUISITELY RENDERED SCENES FROM NATURE. SHOREBIRDS ON THE MANTEL ARE BY LONG ISLAND DECOY MAKER BILL BOWMAN. THE BROADBILL DUCK DECOY WAS MADE BY LEM WARD OF MARYLAND. THE CANADA GOOSE WITH A NOTCHED NECK IS A SPECIAL FAVORITE.

N OVEMBER, A
BOATING SCENE BY PLEISSNER,
OVERLOOKS A TABLE OF
SHOREBIRDS FROM NANTUCKET
AND A WOOD DUCK CARVED BY
TOM CHAMBERS. ON THE BASKET,
A NEW ENGLAND SKUNK-HEAD
SCOTER REVEALS THE SENSITIVE
TOUCH OF AN ANONYMOUS
CRAFTSMAN. MANY EARLY
AMERICAN DECOYS ARE UNSIGNED
WORKS DIFFICULT TO ATTRIBUTE TO
INDIVIDUALS BUT USUALLY
IDENTIFIABLE BY REGION.

SHOREBIRDS UNDER THE GAME BOARD IN THE DINING ROOM, *LEFT*, ARE BY JOHN DILLEY OF QUOGUE, NEW YORK. TWO PAIRS OF CANVASBACK DUCK DECOYS ON THE BOTTOM SHELF WERE MADE BY LEM WARD IN 1936. AN OIL STILL LIFE BY R. LEBARRE GOODWIN IS THE BACKDROP FOR AN OUTSTANDING COLLECTION OF SHOREBIRDS AND DUCK DECOYS IN THE DINING ROOM, *BELOW.* ON THE MANTEL, SHOREBIRDS BY ELMER CROWELL, CAPE COD'S MASTER CARVER, FLANK TWO OF THE ORIGINAL BROAD-BILL DUCKS BELONGING TO THE "CENTENNIAL RIG" CREATED BY BEN HOLMES OF STRATFORD, CONNECTICUT. A FRIENDLY PRESENCE ON ONE SIDE TABLE IN THE DINING ROOM, *RIGHT*, CONSISTS OF A BLACK DUCK DECOY BY THE LEGENDARY CHARLES "SHANG" WHEELER OF STRATFORD, A NANTUCKET BASKET FILLED WITH CARVED WOOD FRUIT, AND AN EARLY EFFORT IN DONAL O'BRIEN'S LIFELONG ENTHUSIASM FOR DECOY CARVING, A GREEN-WINGED TEAL THAT WON A BLUE RIBBON AT THE U.S. NATIONAL DECOY CONTEST.

THE FACE-OFF ON THE MANTELPIECE, *LEFT,* IS BETWEEN A GROUP OF SHOREBIRDS WITH WHALEBONE BILLS, MADE BEFORE THE CIVIL WAR, BY THE FOGLER FAMILY, EARLY SETTLERS ON NANTUCKET AND A FAMOUS WHALING FAMILY, AND TURN-OF-THE-CENTURY SHOREBIRDS BY BILL BOWMAN AND LOTHROP HOLMES. OGDEN PLEISSNER'S *NORTHEAST SALT POND* DEPICTS ONE OF THE O'BRIEN FAMILY'S FAVORITE DUCK-HUNTING LOCATIONS ON THE ISLAND. OVER THE ANTIQUE AMERICAN SLANT-TOP DESK, *RIGHT,* IS ROLAND CLARK'S DRAMATIC PAINTING *BREAK OF DAY PINTAILS. BELOW,* TWO "PINCHED-BREAST" PINTAILS BY LEM WARD OVERLOOK A PAIR OF CANVASBACK DECOYS BY J. WELLS.

EVEN THE KITCHEN OF THIS SPORTING FAMILY IS ALIVE WITH FOLK ART RENDERINGS OF WILDLIFE, INCLUDING A RARE CARVING OF AN ATLANTIC SALMON BY SHANG WHEELER, WHO IS BETTER KNOWN FOR HIS WATERFOWL DECOYS; AN ASSEMBLAGE OF FISH DECOYS ONCE USED TO LURE LAKE FISH TO FISHING HOLES CUT IN THE ICE IN WINTER, AND THE FLYING PINTAIL CARVED BY IRA HUDSON WITH ENTHUSIASM AND SKILL. CARACARA HAWKS ARE DEPICTED IN A PRINT FROM THE MONUMENTAL SERIES BY JOHN JAMES AUDUBON.

THE BREAKFAST ROOM FEATURES A WATERCOLOR STUDY BY OGDEN PLEISSNER FOR THE PAINTING *NORTHEAST SALT POND,* ELSEWHERE IN THE HOUSE, AND AN EVOCATIVE PORTRAIT OF A SOLITARY FISHERMAN BY THOMAS AQUINAS DALY (SEE PAGES 116–117), A CONTEMPORARY ARTIST WHOM DONAL O'BRIEN ADMIRES FOR HIS "TECHNICAL SKILL AND HIS SENSITIVITY AS AN OUTDOORSMAN."

SHOOTING IN THE LOW COUNTRY

Woodhaven represents an Atlanta family's successful efforts to build anew on a century-old tradition in the Low Country of south Georgia.

"We wanted the house to have all the qualities and details of a traditional quail plantation," says Mickey Loudermilk, whose husband, Charles, also intended for it to serve as the base of his ambitious cattle operation featuring the French Limousine breed.

Mickey and her daughter, Lisa Carter, designed the house, which was completed in 1969, with the help of architect Jack Wilson and located some of its most dramatic furnishings, such as the large paintings of the Royal Hounds of Louis XIV, on trips to southern France and the English Cotswolds.

IN THE CLASSIC ANTEBELLUM DESIGN FORGED BY A PROTÉGÉ OF ARCHITECT WILLIAM FRANK MCCALL, JR., DETAILS OF HOME, SUCH AS DEEP PORCHES FRONT AND BACK AND A DINNER BELL, *ABOVE*, INSPIRED BY A FAVORITE LOCAL QUARRY, HAVE NOT BEEN FORSAKEN. THE CARVED LIMESTONE LINTELS OVER THE WINDOWS WERE MADE IN MACON, GEORGIA. *BELOW*, THE TRADITIONAL SHOOTING WAGON ARRIVES TO PICK UP GUESTS FOR A DAY IN THE FIELD.

"We insisted on wraparound porches to give the house the Low Country feeling appropriate for this part of Georgia," Mickey explains. "All the carpenters, craftsmen, and artists who contributed to the building come from this area."

The Loudermilks consider Woodhaven still a work in progress, but it has already achieved a comfortable sporting character time can only improve.

ABRACE OF QUAIL, *ABOVE,* CARVED BY DON ROLLAND OF SYLVESTER, GEORGIA, ENLIVENS THE MANTELPIECE IN THE FAMILY DEN, *CENTER LEFT.* THE ENTRANCE HALL FEATURES A DOME MURAL, *TOP LEFT,* PAINTED BY RANDY GIBBS OF MOULTRIE, AND AN 18TH-CENTURY HUNT SCENE, *BOTTOM LEFT,* FROM THE SCHOOL OF DEPORTE.

A SPACIOUS REAR HALLWAY ALSO SERVES AS A CONVENIENT GUN ROOM FOR FRIENDS AND GUESTS WHO VISIT WOODHAVEN FOR DOVE SHOOTS IN THE FALL AND QUAIL AND DUCK HUNTS IN THE WINTER. CHARLES LOUDERMILK HAS HUNTED WITH THE SAME GROUP OF FRIENDS IN SOUTH GEORGIA FOR 40 YEARS. HIS SON, DAVID, HAS HUNTED SINCE HE WAS A BOY, WHILE DAUGHTERS LISA AND LINDA AND DAUGHTER-IN-LAW, FRANCES, HAVE ALL BECOME GOOD SHOTS SINCE WOODHAVEN OPENED. MICKEY LOUDERMILK ENJOYS WATCHING THE HUNTSMEN AND DOGS FROM HER HORSE OR RIDING ON THE MULE WAGON.

FLOATING SCULPTURE

Carved wildfowl decoys are a unique American art form and, like jazz, they have flourished in a wide range of regional variations—corresponding to major flyways used by ducks and geese in their annual migrations. The virtuosos of the art are legendary carvers like Elmer Crowell on Cape Cod, Joseph Lincoln, Ira Hudson, the Ward Brothers on the Eastern Shore, and—one of the most prolific—"Maker Unknown."

Today, an 85-year-old retired New England sea captain personifies the most endearing aspects of the bird-carving tradition. Cap'n Smith makes working decoys for his own use and pleasure, each Christmas shipping off his latest creations to children, grandchildren, and great-grandchildren.

"I just enjoy it," he says, "and I also think, in a small way, the ducks will be my way of surviving in the world, long after I'm dead and gone."

CAP'N SMITH, *RIGHT,* PURSUES DECOY-MAKING WITH AN EQUANIMITY BORN OF MORE THAN A HALF CENTURY OF DUCK HUNTING, REMINDERS OF WHICH, *LEFT,* ARE NEVER FAR FROM HIS LATEST CREATION. CARVED BIRDS WERE STRICTLY OF LOCAL INTEREST UNTIL JOEL BARBER PUBLISHED HIS COMPREHENSIVE STUDY, *WILDFOWL DECOYS.* THE BOOK HELPED TO VALIDATE "AMERICAN FLOATING SCULPTURE" AS A LEGITIMATE ART FORM.

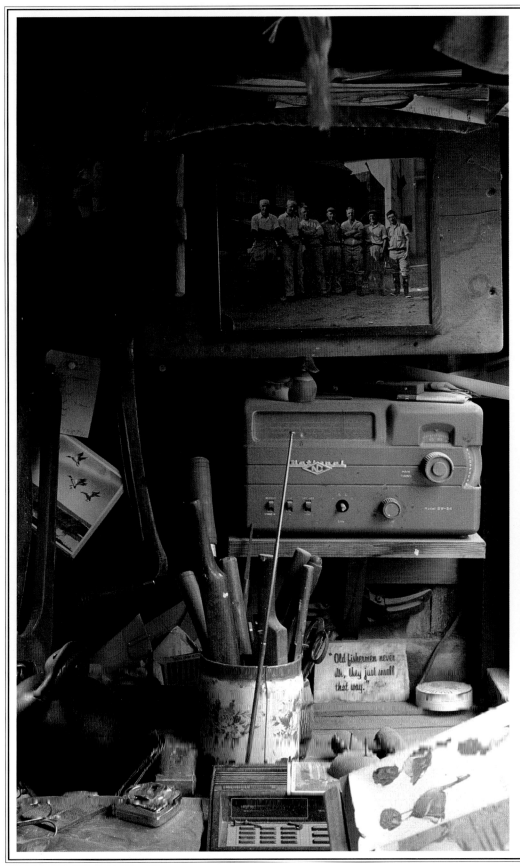

To MAKE A DECOY, CAP'N SMITH HOLLOWS OUT TWO PIECES OF NATIVE PINE, THEN GLUES AND CLAMPS THEM INTO A BLOCK, ONTO WHICH HE TRACES THE DUCK. HE CUTS THE ROUGH SHAPE ON HIS BAND SAW, THEN USES A DRAW KNIFE TO SHAPE THE BODY. THE DUCK HEAD IS CARVED OUT OF ANOTHER PINE PIECE, THEN SCREWED TO THE BODY. FINALLY, THE DECOY IS PAINTED WITH FLAT OIL-BASED COLORS.

LAB HEAVEN

Borderline Plantation, in the rolling red clay and sand hills of northern Florida, is home to Labrador retrievers and myriad likenesses of Labs and other animals in various forms.

"The sounds, smells, and sights of nature have been part of my life for as long as I can remember," says Sallie Sullivan, who made the outdoors as important as the interiors when she built her house in 1974. "I doubt there's anything as exciting or beautiful as the whistling of ring-necked ducks as they set their wings to come into a pond before sunrise."

Labs are traditionally used to retrieve bobwhite quail on the hunts that take place over the winter months on the numerous plantations in the area. "For me, the dogs and horses involved with the hunt are the most important part," she says. She doesn't really enjoy hunting unless it involves trained animals. "I want to shoot well for the dogs."

SALLIE TRAVELS EXTENSIVELY EVERY YEAR WITH HOME-BRED, HOME-TRAINED BIRDIE, BEAST, CARRY, AND CARBON, *BELOW,* EXHIBITING THEM IN FIELD TRIALS WITH NOTABLE SUCCESS. A LIFELONG SPORTSWOMAN, SHE COLLECTS PAINTINGS AND SCULPTURE, *RIGHT,* "BECAUSE THEY BRING BACK MEMORIES OF HUNTS OR PLACES."

MORE THAN THE RIBBONS HER MASTER HUNTERS HAVE WON, OR THE PINS SHE HAS COLLECTED, SALLIE SULLIVAN APPRECIATES "THE JOY THE DOGS THEMSELVES GET FROM FIELD TRIALS, AND FOR ME, THE MOST FUN IS SEEING THE PRIDE AND LOVE SHARED BETWEEN THE DOGS AND THEIR OWNERS." SHE ADDS, "I OFTEN SAY I GO TO A GREAT DEAL OF TROUBLE TO ENTERTAIN MY LABS. FITTING FOUR OF THEM INTO MY STATION WAGON CAN BE A CHALLENGE, BUT IN FACT THEY ARE GOOD TRAVELERS AND ARE POSITIVELY JOYOUS WHEN THEY ARE COMPETING."

WATERFOWL FESTIVAL

The Waterfowl Festival attracts over 20,000 visitors to the colonial town of Easton, on Maryland's Eastern Shore, every year under fall skies filled with boisterous formations of migrating Canada geese. Visitors arrive from all over the Eastern seaboard for this one-of-a-kind event.

In a friendly street-fair atmosphere, bird lovers come to view and purchase waterfowl art, carvings, duck-stamp prints, antique and newly carved decoys, books, and other wildfowling artifacts from around the world. They soak in the autumn hunt scene exhibits in shop windows and sample local fare such as crab soup, fried clams, freshly shucked oysters from the Chesapeake, and "Miss Mary's Famous Chicken Salad" from Hill's Drug Store.

RETRIEVER DEMONSTRATIONS ON THE BAY STREET POND, *BELOW,* DURING FESTIVAL WEEKEND CELEBRATE THE SKILLS OF PRIZED LABRADORS, GOLDENS, AND CHESAPEAKE BAYS. ON PAPER MILL POND, *RIGHT,* A SHORT WALK FROM EASTON'S CENTER, ONE OF AUTUMN'S FIRST MIGRATING FLOCKS OF CANADA GEESE COMES TO ROOST UNDER THE COVER OF DUSK.

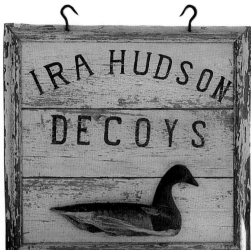

WITH STREETS CLOSED TO TRAFFIC TO MAKE WAY FOR OYSTER SHUCKERS AND OTHER VENDORS, AND THE FIREHOUSE, THE ELKS CLUB, THE GENTEEL TIDEWATER INN, AND EVEN TWO CHURCHES CONVERTED TO VENUES FOR WORKSHOPS, ART EXHIBITS, AND SWAP MEETS, EASTON GIVES ITSELF OVER ALMOST ENTIRELY TO WATERFOWL MANIA FOR THREE DAYS EVERY NOVEMBER. LIKE MALCOLM BAHRENBURG, *LEFT*, AND HIS FRIENDS IN THE TALBOT RETRIEVER CLUB OF MARYLAND, WILDFOWLERS AREN'T SHY ABOUT EXHIBITING THEIR FAVORITE PURSUITS AND AFFILIATIONS.

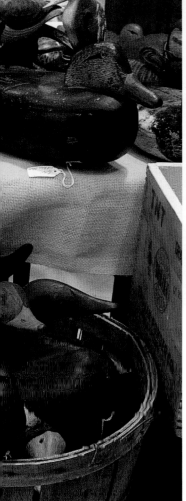

The festival coincides with the opening of hunting season, so it's a time when burly, bearded fellows in green-and-brown camouflage gear may stand on the corner, holding shotguns, and nobody panics. Dogs are as welcome in hotels and shops as they are in the retriever demonstrations conducted on the town pond, or at the auctions, duck-calling contests, and swap meets.

One store sells a telephone shaped like a duck during the weekend of the Waterfowl Festival. When a call comes in, the phone quacks.

CARL BECKER, *LEFT,* AND HUNDREDS OF OTHER CARVERS AND WILDLIFE ARTISTS COME TO TOWN TO DEMONSTRATE THEIR CRAFT AND SELL THEIR WARES. COMMISSIONS COLLECTED ON ALL SALES MADE AT THE FESTIVAL HAVE ENABLED ORGANIZERS TO CONTRIBUTE MORE THAN TWO MILLION DOLLARS TO THE PRESERVATION OF NATIVE AND MIGRATING WATERFOWL POPULATIONS

TEXAS SHOOTING PARTY

"Some of the closest friendships are made in the field," says Virginia Elverson. She and her English-born husband, Robin, spend weekends in a 150-year-old compound of Bavarian-style farmhouse buildings in the Texas hill country. In the surrounding countryside of rolling meadows and meandering creeks, woods of oak and cedar, and thickets of wild plum, grape, and blackberry vines, the Elversons shoot dove, duck, goose, and quail in the fall and winter months.

When they bought the farm twenty-five years ago, Robin discovered hunting with a Texas accent. "Having grown up in the British tradition of shooting with the assistance of gamekeepers, beaters, and

THE VIEW FROM THE BACK PORCH OF THE MAIN HOUSE, *RIGHT,* ENCOMPASSES ROLLING HILLS FULL OF DEER, RABBITS, THE OCCASIONAL WOLF, AND A GREAT VARIETY OF BIRD LIFE. THE FARM'S OUTBUILDINGS PROVIDE THE HUMAN CHARACTER. IN THE ONE-ROOM COOK HOUSE, *ABOVE AND BELOW,* BUILT IN 1860, VIRGINIA PRACTICES OLD-TIME COOKERY USING SUCH IMPLEMENTS AS THE "ROASTING KITCHEN," A BARREL-SHAPED TIN DEVICE THAT ONCE FUNCTIONED AS A KIND OF HEARTHSIDE MICROWAVE.

TEXAS'S WIDE-OPEN SPACES SUGGEST A HUNTER'S PARADISE, BUT IN FACT MOST GAME IS PURSUED IN THIS STATE ON PRIVATELY OWNED LAND BY PERMIT ONLY. ON THE MORNING OF A DOVE HUNT, HOLLAND & HOLLAND SIDE-BY-SIDE SHOTGUNS, INCLUDING A TURN-OF-CENTURY MODEL THAT BELONGED TO ROBIN'S FATHER, MAJOR JAMES HAMILTON ELVERSON, STAND READY FOR ACTION AMID CAMOUFLAGE GEAR. "AT OUR FARM WE CAN GO INTO THE FIELD AT ANY TIME," VIRGINIA ELVERSON OBSERVES. "SHOOTING IS NOT A PLANNED ACTIVITY BUT SOMETHING WE DO SPUR OF THE MOMENT."

ENGLISH LEATHER SHOOTING CASES AND AN OLD SHOOTING STICK HAVE FOUND A PLACE IN THE INFORMAL HUNT TRADITIONS OF THE ELVERSON FARM, ALONGSIDE HIDE-BOTTOM CHAIRS. THE FARM BUILDINGS' *FACHWERK* CONSTRUCTION DATES FROM THE MID TO LATE 19TH CENTURY, WHEN A LARGE GERMAN POPULATION EMIGRATED TO THE TEXAS HILL COUNTRY.

103

loaders, it was a real adjustment for him," Virginia recalls with a laugh. "Hooking clothes—and skin— on barbed-wire fences while dove shooting, lying flat on his back clad in white in a wet rice field to avoid detection by the geese, or bouncing across the prairie in a Jeep to keep up with dogs tracking quail—all were new shooting customs for Robin, and, he admits, great fun!"

Virginia is an antiques collector, cookbook author, and cooking teacher, so it was inevitable that these and her sporting interests combined to stamp a distinctive atmosphere on the ranch and enliven the couple's menus for "company" with such delectable recipes as pan-fried quail with kümmel and walnuts, and grilled breast of dove with jalapeño.

AN AIRY ROOM, *LEFT,* WITH EARLY TEXAS BEDS FASHIONED FROM NATIVE CEDAR AND PINE, IS A WELCOME REFUGE AFTER A DAWN PATROL IN SEARCH OF DOVE OR QUAIL. AN OLD PHOTOGRAPH OF THE WHITTLEY FAMILY ABOVE LIVING AS A TRIBUTE TO THE GERMAN SETTLERS WHO FIRST HOMESTEADED ON THE ELVERSONS' FARM IN THE 1840S, AND A DEERSKIN RUG, HELP TO GIVE THE HOUSE THE DISTINCTIVE CHARACTER OF THE RURAL HILL COUNTRY IN TEXAS.

SHOOTING ON THE MARSH

There are sixty or more prime shooting locations in the 2,300 acres of marshland owned by the 120-year-old Ottawa Shooting Club near Cleveland, Ohio (a neighbor of Winous Point Shooting Club, pages 72–75), and some are more bountiful than others. Every night before dinner during hunting season, in front of a roaring fire in the clubhouse, each member rolls the dice to determine his duck blind the following day.

"There is always a lot of chatter about sites, prior to the draw," notes club president Dickson L. Whitney, "with the hope that you can conceal a location you believe no one else knows about but which you feel will be very productive."

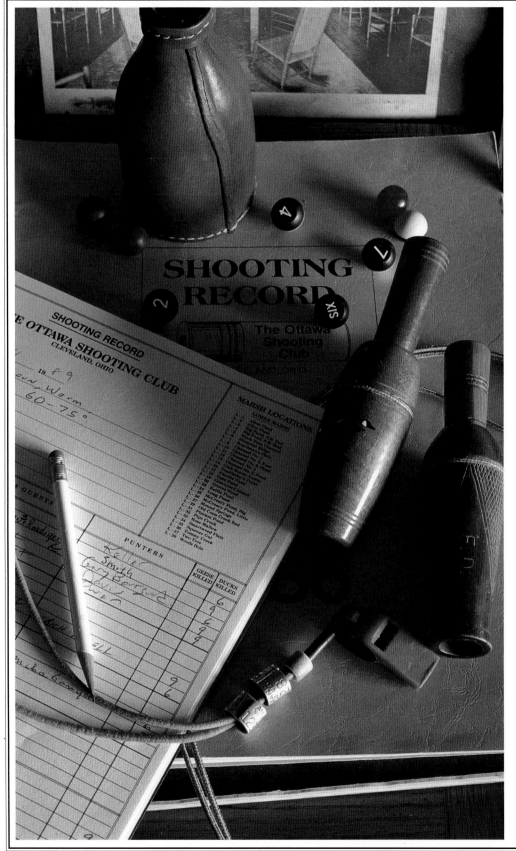

A DRAW FROM THE DICE BOX, *LEFT,* DETERMINES THE ORDER IN WHICH OTTAWA'S MEMBERS PICK THEIR DUCK BLINDS. THE CLUB'S RECORD BOOK SHOWS WHERE THE BEST SHOOTING HAS OCCURRED IN THE PAST, BUT WIND, WEATHER, WATER, AND FOOD CONDITIONS MAKE EACH FALL-WINTER HUNTING SEASON SOMEWHAT UNPREDICTABLE. THE MARSH IS A BEAUTIFUL PRESERVE, *ABOVE AND OPPOSITE.*

OTTAWA'S
OVERNIGHT LODGING CONSISTS
OF ROOMS INDIVIDUALLY OWNED
BY MEMBERS AND FURNISHED
ACCORDING TO THEIR PERSONAL
STYLE, OR NONSTYLE, AND WHICH
ARE INVARIABLY EQUIPPED WITH A
DUCK HUNTER'S ESSENTIAL GEAR.

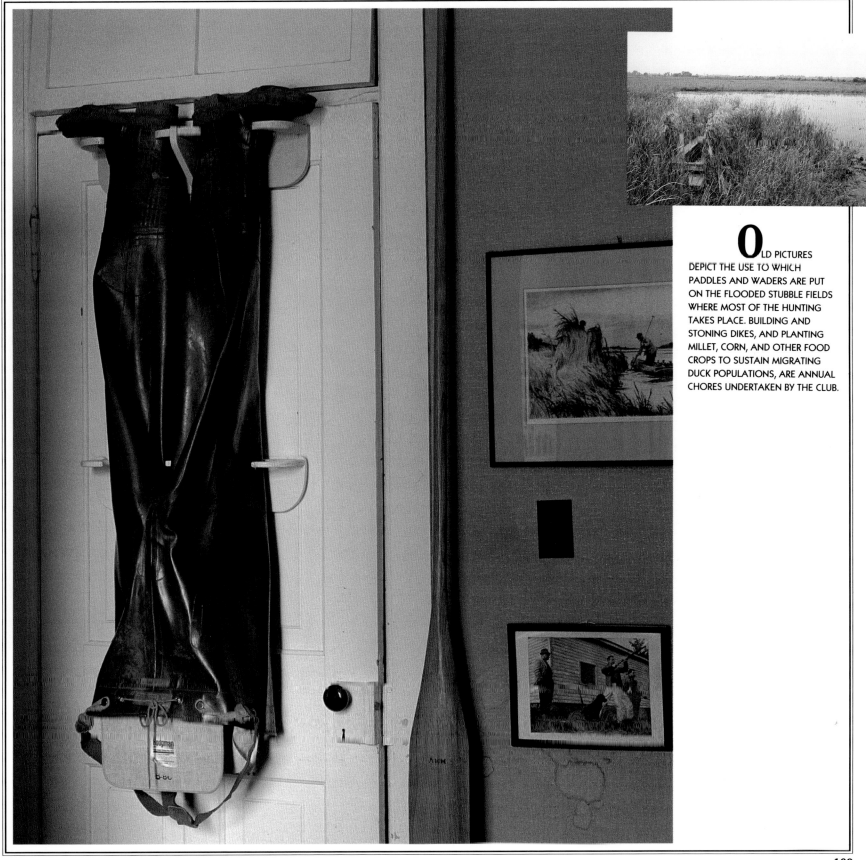

OLD PICTURES
DEPICT THE USE TO WHICH
PADDLES AND WADERS ARE PUT
ON THE FLOODED STUBBLE FIELDS
WHERE MOST OF THE HUNTING
TAKES PLACE. BUILDING AND
STONING DIKES, AND PLANTING
MILLET, CORN, AND OTHER FOOD
CROPS TO SUSTAIN MIGRATING
DUCK POPULATIONS, ARE ANNUAL
CHORES UNDERTAKEN BY THE CLUB.

ROMANCE OF THE QUAIL HUNT

There is nothing quite like it on our sporting scene, "refined and even elegant traditions on one hand, and the rough-and-tumble of nature as encountered by the bird hunter on the other," observes Charlie Chapin, speaking of his life at Elsoma, the house he, wife Jeanie, and family built in the long-leaf pine woodlands near Thomasville, Georgia, in 1964. The sport of shooting quail involves exquisitely managed wildlife habitat, fancy shotguns, wonderful bird dogs and retrievers, lumbering old hand-built shooting wagons, mules and horses, and feisty Jack Russell terriers thrown in for good measure.

BOTH THE MAIN HOUSE, WITH ITS COLUMNED PORCH, TALL CHIMNEYS, AND ROOFLINE, *BELOW,* AND THE GUEST COTTAGE, *LEFT,* AT ELSOMA REFLECT ELEMENTS OF STYLE INDIGENOUS TO THE SOUTH GEORGIA AREA. PUNCH, THE RESIDENT JACK TERRIER, *ABOVE,* BELONGS TO A BREED THAT THINKS IT IS MUCH BIGGER THAN IT REALLY IS.

B ELGIAN HORSES, RATHER THAN MULES, ARE USED TO PULL THE SHOOTING BUGGY TO THE HUNT AT ELSOMA. POINTERS WORK IN PAIRS AS THEY SEEK OUT COVEYS OF QUAIL IN THE PINEY WOODS. CHARLIE CHAPIN'S UNIQUE KENNEL FOR HIS DOGS UTILIZES 20 DISCARDED JACK DANIELS WHISKEY BARRELS AND TERRA-COTTA BASES. "EACH DOG HOUSE COST ABOUT TEN DOLLARS," HE REPORTS, "AND HAS NO CORNER FOR A DOG TO START HIS CHEWING, IS HIGH AND OUT OF THE WAY OF URINE TRAJECTORY, AND TAKES UP LITTLE GROUND SPACE, ALLOWING THE DOG TO MOVE ABOUT OR LIE UNDERNEATH."

A couple of hundred quail plantations, some grandiose and rather dull, others commercial and rather small, exist on the former hunting grounds of the Creek and Apalachee Indians along the Florida Georgia border. Elsoma is representive of the best of them. "Nature keeps the game unpredictable, saving it from becoming ritual alone," says Chapin. "But tradition enriches the pursuit of quarry, and success becomes a measure, not of the day's bag, but of the totality of the experience." The chance to work with dogs is the most pleasing aspect of the quail hunt for Chapin, and his all-time favorite, a pointer named Man, is buried within a few paces of Elsoma. "He was difficult and frustrating to train," Charlie recalls, "but he became a great dog, winning field trials, and outlived every other pointer we ever had. So I decided he deserved a special burial, at 15½ years, and an accurate epitaph: 'Old Son of a Bitch.' "

BOTH THE AUDUBON PRINT AND THE FIRE SCREEN IN THE LIVING ROOM, *LEFT*, ARE REMINDERS OF LOCAL WILDLIFE SPECIES. IN THE DINING ROOM, *ABOVE*, THE CENTER OF ATTRACTION IS A PAINTING OF THE ANNUAL GEORGIA-FLORIDA FIELD TRIAL BY PETER CORBIN. *BELOW*, SPENT SHOTGUN SHELLS ADD A SPORTING TOUCH TO A WINDOW SHADE, ALONG WITH THE "GEORGIA BUGGY," THE VEHICLE OF CHOICE FOR SHOOTING IN QUAIL PLANTATION COUNTRY.

WHEN TOM DALY
IS NOT WORKING IN HIS STUDIO
UPSTAIRS IN THE BARN, HE IS
LIKELY TO BE BOW HUNTING FOR
WHITETAIL DEER, ICE FISHING FOR
WALLEYE AND PERCH, CALLING
IN WILD TURKEY, RUNNING A
TRAPLINE, HUNTING DUCKS FROM
A SNEAKBOAT ON LAKE ERIE
("ABSOLUTE MURDER IN THE
WINTER"), OR WATCHING HIS TWIN
BOYS PLAY LITTLE LEAGUE
BASEBALL. HE ESCHEWS THE NEW
YORK ART GALLERY SCENE,
PREFERRING THE "RURAL POETRY"
OF HIS LIFE AND ART.

A SPORTING ARTIST

Thomas Aquinas Daly draws on his lifelong passion for hunting, fishing, and the natural environment to create still lifes and landscapes that imbue the sporting scene with what one critic has called "a natural sanctity and integrity." He paints in the same barn in Arcade, New York, where he ties flies, makes arrows, and carves his decoys, and his canvases have the unsentimental character of the region and the uncompromising quality of his ethical approach to the chase. "I like to stay with the old traditions," he says, "augmenting the role of human skills and shrinking the role of gadgets." Since 1970, when Daly left a career as a lithographer and art director to become a serious painter, he has been "constantly bombarded with visuals" in his luminescent world of ponds and streams, flowers and sky, wildlife and weather, the hunter and the hunted.

THE MOODY REALISM PERVASIVE IN DALY'S WORK, *RIGHT,* AND DISTINCTIVELY HIS OWN ALSO INFORMS MORE PROSAIC OBJECTS SUCH AS HIS RIG OF DECOYS, *FAR RIGHT,* WHICH THE ARTIST CARVED AND PAINTED HIMSELF. ONCE, HAVING LEFT THE RIG FLOATING UNATTENDED NOT FAR FROM SHORE, DALY RETURNED JUST IN TIME TO OBSERVE TWO OTHER HUNTERS OPEN FIRE ON THE WOODEN DUCKS. "I GUESS I CARVED THEM PRETTY GOOD," HE MODESTLY NOTES.

A TIMELESS SPELL

El Destino is only about twelve miles from Tallahassee, the bustling capital of Florida, but sometimes it feels hundreds of years away in time. The home of native Floridians Sandy and Melinda Proctor and their three children, this plantation reverberates with Indian, Spanish, and Old South heritage. "It's like being in some primeval place," says Sandy, a sporting artist who grew up absorbing the hunting traditions of the South from his father and friends. "I used to go out coon hunting at night with a plantation hand named Elijah Lamb," he recalls.

LIVE OAKS LINING THE ENTRANCE, *OPPOSITE*, WERE PLANTED 150 YEARS AGO WHEN U.S. ARMY OFFICER AND DIPLOMAT JAMES GADSEN OWNED EL DESTINO. THE PRESENT HOUSE, *ABOVE*, WAS DESIGNED IN 1935 BY NEW YORK ARCHITECT BURRAL HOFFMAN. IN THE ENTRY HALL, *RIGHT*, ARE SANDY PROCTOR'S BRONZE SCULPTURE, *MANATEE*, AND HAND-TINTED PRINTS OF BIRDS OF PREY FROM FRANCE.

A NTIQUE DOORS AND CORBELS, *ABOVE,* WERE COLLECTED IN SPAIN AND LATIN AMERICA TO EMBELLISH THE SUNKEN 37-FOOT-LONG LIVING ROOM, *BELOW.* DESKTOP PORTRAITS, *RIGHT,* SHOW SANDY AND SON STANLEY IN A SNEAKBOAT ON LAKE IAMONIA, SON STEWART WITH HIS FIRST WHITE TAIL DEER, AND SANDY AND FRIENDS IN AN ARKANSAS DUCK BLIND. *PRAIRIE WINGS,* BY RICHARD BISHOP AND EDGAR M. QUEENY, IS A CLASSIC PEN-AND-CAMERA STUDY OF DUCKS IN FLIGHT, WHICH WAS FIRST PUBLISHED IN 1946.

"He taught me how to work my way through the swamp without stepping in the potholes, and the different strains to listen for in the voices of the dogs to determine whether they were on the trail of a raccoon or a bobcat. Elijah was devoutly religious and if it was Saturday night, he'd put out our campfire before midnight and we'd walk home. He wouldn't hunt on Sunday." The earliest known inhabitants of the land at El Destino were the Apalachee Indians. The Spaniards arrived in 1655 and established a large Franciscan mission, which burned in a raid and massacre by the Creek Indians and the English in 1703. Just before the Civil War, El Destino grew to a 7,000-acre cotton plantation with fifty-eight slaves and their families, thirty-three plows, and nineteen mules. Eventually the plantation declined, with the original home and other buildings lost to fire, but it obtained a new lease on life in the 1930s, when the present manor house, stables, and other buildings were built as a hunting plantation. The Proctors acquired the land recently, renovated the stables, and adapted one of the outbuildings for Sandy's painting and sculpture studio, but are otherwise determined to keep the ghosts of El Destino intact, and friendly.

THE ANTLERS OF A
SIX-POINT ELK FROM BRITISH
COLUMBIA DOMINATE THE ARTIST'S
STUDIO, *LEFT,* WHERE AN OIL
PAINTING OF ELEPHANTS IN TSAVO,
EAST AFRICA, IS IN PROGRESS. IN
THE GUN ROOM, *RIGHT,* AN OLD
FISHING CREEL, A HANDWOVEN
INDIAN RUG, AND AN AFRICAN
MEDICINE BAG HAVE MADE
THEMSELVES AT HOME.

GRAVEN IMAGES

Master gun engraver Winston Churchill, a seventh-generation Vermonter, sees hunting and fishing as "an oasis of truth in lives that otherwise have become distant, highly technical, and artificial." As a youth, he became fascinated with the tools and weapons used in hunting. That, together with a gift for art, led him into gunsmithing, stockmaking, and eventually a career in engraving. The microscopic beauty and fidelity to nature in Churchill's work is widely known, and one knowledgeable observer claims that "he may be the finest craftsman in this century to engrave a gun." A pertinent quotation from John Ruskin occupies a prominent place in Churchill's house. "When we build," it begins, "let us think that we build forever. . . ."

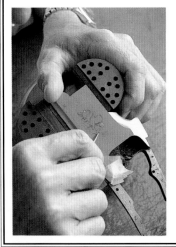

USING ONLY A SIMPLE HAND TOOL CALLED THE GRAVER, GUIDED BY A HUMAN HAND PRACTICED IN THE CENTURIES-OLD TECHNIQUES OF HIS CRAFT, WINSTON CHURCHILL TRANSFORMS AN ALREADY EXPENSIVE FIREARM INTO A WORK OF ART, *LEFT AND RIGHT*. SOME COMMISSIONS TAKE A FULL YEAR TO COMPLETE.

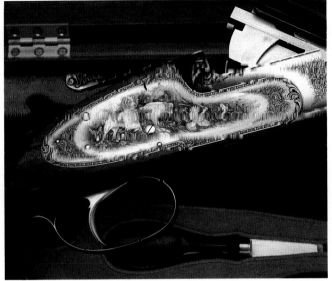

BOTH THE WORKING SKETCH OF A BULL ELEPHANT, *LEFT,* AND ITS REALIZATION ON THE PISTOL GRIP OF A BIG-GAME RIFLE REVEAL THE ARTIST'S SKILL IN PRECISELY RENDERING A MONUMENTAL FIGURE IN A TINY SPACE. A FINISHED PIECE, *ABOVE,* SHOWS BRITTANY SPANIELS FLUSHING RUFFED GROUSE ON THE SIDEPLATE OF A FABBRI 20 GAUGE OVER-AND-UNDER SHOTGUN. ONE INADVERTENT SLIP WITH THE ENGRAVING TOOL, *RIGHT,* WOULD IRREPARABLY DAMAGE THE PIECE.

MASTERS OF THE CHASE

In the New England farmhouse of a couple who have pursued sport all their lives, a collection of paintings, drawings, and carved birds has come to signify the ultimate form of the chase. The husband began grouse and pheasant shooting on his family's farm in Pennsylvania at age eight, and spent summers fishing for bass and bluefish and digging clams on Fisher's Island in Long Island Sound. His wife's earliest recollections are of her father, "a religious grouse hunter," setting forth with his setter, Freckles, every fall weekend in Connecticut's Naugatuck Valley. The woman's experience as a designer readily shows in the way she has brought together the New England antiques and the sporting art assembled by the two of them over the years. The

A PAIR OF LESSER YELLOWLEGS, *LEFT,* CARVED BY ELMER CROWELL IN 1920, MARK TIME NEXT TO A PILLAR-AND-SCROLL SHELF CLOCK BUILT BY ELI TERRY IN ABOUT 1810. TO THE LEFT OF THE FIREPLACE HANGS *SETTING POINTING WOODCOCK,* BY ARTHUR FITZWILLIAM TAIT, 1863; TO THE RIGHT, *NEW ENGLAND FARM BY WINTER ROAD,* BY GEORGE HENRY DURRIE, 1854. THE ENGLISH FIREBOARD HAS AN AFTER-HUNT SCENE.

farmhouse was built in 1835, then rebuilt after a fire in 1850. The couple moved into the place in 1979, adding nothing to the exterior but installing architectural elements such as corner cupboards, paneling, chair rails, and mantels to coordinate with the periods of their furniture collection. Their art collection started with working decoys and Derrydale books, then A. B. Frost prints and drawings, and most recently, original works by such painters as Frank Benson, Carl Rungius, Frederic Remington, and Arthur Fitzwilliam Tait. "Our original attraction was simply to collect images of those activities we enjoyed doing and could relate to," says the woman. "Now we collect sporting art because we feel many of these sports are things of the past. The art is what's left to remind us of them." A few years ago, the man donated his collection of over 200 decoys to a local historical society. Such was his emotional attachment to the "truth and honesty" of these early decoys that he found it nearly unbearable to attend the special exhibit the society proudly arranged to show off its new acquisitions.

ABOVE LEFT, IN A LIVING ROOM ANCHORED BY A CHERRY SLANT-TOP DESK MADE IN CONNECTICUT IN ABOUT 1780, THE PAINTINGS *YELLOW PERCH AND BREEM*, ATTRIBUTED TO W. A. WALKER, CIRCA 1860, AND *THE ADIRONDACKS' LONG LAKE*, BY TAIT, 1873, EVOKE UNBUSINESSLIKE PURSUITS. THE DELFT SALMON BOWL, MADE IN BRISTOL, ENGLAND, IN THE 1750S, IS A RARE EARLY FISH PLATE. *LEFT*, EVEN THE KITCHEN IS RICH IN DETAIL, IN WHAT THE OWNER DESCRIBES AS "A TYPICAL VERMONT FARMHOUSE, WHICH MEANS IT GOES ON AND ON, RAMBLING WITHOUT RHYME OR REASON."

A DRAKE WIDGEON
DECOY WITH WINGS ALOFT, *LEFT*,
CARVED BY IRA HUDSON IN ABOUT
1918, APPARENTLY TO SETTLE A
DENTIST'S BILL, IS ONE OF THIS
SPORTING FAMILY'S MOST PRIZED
POSSESSIONS, SERVING AS THE
CENTERPIECE FOR HOLIDAY FEASTS
IN ALL SEASONS. *GOING OUT* WAS
PAINTED BY TAIT IN 1860.

A MASON BLACK DUCK DECOY, *LEFT,* ROOSTS ON A CONNECTICUT-MADE CHERRY CHIPPENDALE DESK FROM ABOUT THE TIME OF THE REVOLUTION, WHILE TAIT'S *RUFFED GROUSE* REMAIN EVER ALERT. AN ENGLISHMAN, TAIT LIVED AND HUNTED IN THE ADIRONDACKS FOR YEARS, AND HIS ABILITY TO SHOW, BEFORE THE AGE OF THE CAMERA, EVERY TYPICAL MOTION, POSE, COLORATION, AND IDIOSYNCRASY OF WILDLIFE WAS EXCEPTIONAL.

A RECORD-BREAKING TARPON, *FAR RIGHT,* 186 POUNDS, 8 OUNCES, CAUGHT ON A FLY NEAR HOMOSASSA SPRINGS, FLORIDA, BY THE MAN OF THE HOUSE, OCCUPIES A PRIZED PLACE IN HIS IN-HOME OFFICE, DWARFING BONEFISH, SILVER TROPHIES, AND PAPERWORK. TARPON SCALES IN THE LUSTRE BOWL, *RIGHT,* REVEAL A PAPERY BEAUTY SEEMINGLY AT VARIANCE WITH THE BRUTE STRENGTH OF ONE OF THE SPORTING WORLD'S MOST RESPECTED GAME FISH.

A GOOD BIRD DOG MAN

Richard Johns lives in an 18th-century pioneer home in rural Pennsylvania, surrounded by hilly farm fields and half-cleared woods, and by reminders of a lifetime devoted to sporting horses and dogs. His earliest ventures were hunting trips out of the grouse and deer lodges once abundant in the western Poconos. "I learned much about guns, dogs, and game from my uncle and other men who were anxious to see a boy start out right in the shooting and fishing world," he recalls. "That region was a mecca of truly great grouse dogs, of men who knew how to train and handle them and who could shoot grouse as well as anyone in the world." Today, after a half century of success in training and showing

THE WEATHER VANE MADE BY A MARYLAND BLACKSMITH, *ABOVE,* WAS DESIGNED BY RICHARD JOHNS TO COMBINE THE BEST FEATURES OF TWO BIRD DOGS HE ADMIRED, MR. WILLIAM ARKWRIGHT'S SEA BREEZE, THE 1902 ENGLISH CHAMPION (HEAD AND NECK), AND LUMINARY, A MORE RECENT AMERICAN NATIONAL WINNER (BODY AND POINTING STANCE). THE LIVING ROOM, *LEFT,* HAS BECOME THE REPOSITORY FOR NUMEROUS OBJECTS THAT "FRIENDS THINK BELONG THERE," LIKE THE PAINTING OF A YELLOW LABRADOR BY DORIS KAIL. JOHNS'S "SPORTS AFIELD" BUTTON, *RIGHT,* SIGNIFIES THE NAMING OF ONE OF HIS GERMAN SHORTHAIRS TO THE ALL-AMERICAN SPORTING DOG TEAM.

English setters, English pointers, and German shorthairs (a pointer breed he brought back from his military tour of duty in Germany following World War II), Richard has cut back on his schedule. "Field trials are a great deal of fun," he notes, "but they're also hard work, for dog and trainer." He still likes to shoot grouse, woodcock, and quail over good pointing dogs, and to ride and drive good horses; he invites friends over for clay target shooting from time to time; and he still works with a few dogs—there's a kennel next to the building he uses as his office—but no longer travels the field-trial circuit. Watching Johns work with one of his current pointers with a mixture of love, patience, and authority is a privilege; a good bird dog man is hard to find.

DOGS ARE EVERYWHERE IN THE JOHNS HOUSEHOLD. A WEATHERED COPPER SETTER AND POINTER STAND GUARD ON A SHELF, *ABOVE LEFT,* WHILE THE HANDIWORK OF MADGE JOHNS PAYS A HUMBLE TRIBUTE TO THE BEAGLE, A BREED SHE ONCE RAISED, ON A WASTE-BASKET, *LEFT.* SEVERAL MORE ANIMALS HAVE BEEN STOWED UNCEREMONIOUSLY ALONGSIDE AN OLD TROPHY AND A PEWTER TEAPOT IN THE OFFICE, *ABOVE.*

A STEAMED HICKORY HAT RACK, *LEFT*, IS USED TO STORE A GUN CASE, HARNESSES, AND OTHER TACK, INCLUDING RICHARD JOHNS'S MONOGRAMMED DRIVING BRIDLE FOR CARRIAGE HORSES. THE 19TH CENTURY GERMAN AMMUNITION BAG, *BELOW*, IS MADE OF ROEBUCK HIDE AND WOVEN CORD.

THE HUNT

It was in 1650 that Robert Brooke, Esquire, landed in the colony of Saint Mary, with his wife, children, servants, and a pack of English foxhounds. Almost immediately, Brooke began hunting the native gray fox in the tidewater flatlands near present-day Annapolis, Maryland. Thus began a tradition in which Americans would adapt the quintessential English sport of fox hunting to the environment, customs, conditions, and character of the New World.

Today the fox (or, in many locales, the abundant coyote) is hunted in thirty-four states on terrain as varied as our continent has to offer: the open farmland and woods of New England, the piney sandhills and swamps of South Carolina, the "galloping country" of the Texas plains, the mountain meadows of the Colorado Rockies, and the mesas, canyons, and rolling grasslands of southern California. Obstacles to be cleared by horse and rider range from stone walls and chicken coops to

HOUNDS ARE THE LINK BETWEEN FOX HUNTERS AND THE ELUSIVE FOX. THEY LIVE AS A PACK IN A KENNEL AND ARE NOT TREATED AS PETS, EVEN BY NOVICES.

hunting in the rural countryside, amid at times a chaos of sensations and events. Dedicated fox hunters put in hundreds of hours of training and conditioning to perfect their riding skills. As much effort goes into the breeding, training, and maintaining of the hounds by the huntsman, who is a salaried professional, although in many cases it is the master of foxhounds who conducts the hunt.

Fox-hunting etiquette is one of those codes of sportsmanship that committed hunters take very seriously. Some of the most important rules have to do with the farmers and other landowners whose properties, after all, the hunt could not do without. Thus: "If you open a gate, you must shut it." And: "It does not improve wheat (or corn, or soybeans) to ride on it." Other rules of courtesy and safety are for the hunter's own good, and still others entreat him to keep his horse out of the way of the huntsman and hounds as they attempt to "draw a covert" (find a fox in a certain area).

Given the natural pageantry of the hunt and its long history both in this country and Great Britain, it is not surprising to learn it is a sporting pursuit rich in art, artifacts, and accessories. The houses, stables, and tack rooms of fox-hunting families are often graced with treasured possessions handed down over the decades, along with collections of stirrup cups, riding crops, hunting horns, sporting prints, and books on the hunt.

ditches, saddle gates, and fences strung with PVC-covered barbed wire.

There are organized hunts named after Princess Anne, Grandfather Mountain, and Wilbur Ross Hubbard, who has maintained his private pack of hounds, "Mr. Hubbard's Kent County Hounds," on the Eastern Shore of Maryland for more than forty years. One year his pack chased a fox over a recently harvested soybean field and put it to ground in a goose pit, filled at the time with goose hunters. The sport seems to have the same rejuvenating effect on masters of foxhounds as classical music has on conductors. Mr. Hubbard, although well into his nineties, still chases foxes on horseback.

The character of the terrain being hunted and factors of climate, like altitude, dictate to a degree the horse and the horsemanship required of a fox hunter. There is a major difference between riding in a show ring and

THE COLORS AND SYMBOLS OF EVERY ORGANIZED HUNT IN THE UNITED STATES SPEAK TO A PARTICULAR CUSTOM OR TRADITION.

According to J. M. Peters, a director of the Museum of Hounds and Hunting in Leesburg, Virginia, stirrup cups in the likeness of a head of a hound, rabbit, or stag originated in England in the 17th century and were made of clay, porcelain, or silver. The cups got their name from the tradition of offering a bracing dose of spirits to a traveler who had just mounted his horse and was settled in saddle and stirrups, ready to commence the trip. Fox hunters adapted the custom to fortify themselves at the start of a hunt. The hunt board, used to serve food and drink to hunters at the end of an outing, was constructed taller than a conventional sideboard because hunters dismounted from their horses and stood around the board to eat.

The sporting print was first popularized in England in the early 19th century, when artists and publishers began offering hand-colored etchings and aquatints, relatively inexpensive to produce, for sale to the public. Henry Alken was one of the most successful British artists specializing in riding subjects, and newly prosperous American sporting families enthusiastically acquired his and others' work later in the century.

Turner Reuter, Jr., a Middleburg, Virginia, art dealer who writes frequently on sporting art for *Spur* magazine, credits the Derrydale Press, the legendary American publisher of sporting books from 1926 to 1941, with promoting the first high-quality prints of the hunt in this country. Eugene V. Connett III, Derrydale's founder, commissioned artists such as F. B. Voss, Edward Voss, Edwin Megargee, Paul Brown, and Marguerite Kirmse to paint and draw equestrian subjects, from which he produced aquatints in limited editions.

A COLLECTION OF RIDING CROPS SUGGESTS THE SUPERIOR CRAFTS FOSTERED BY THE PURSUIT OF FOXES.

It is well known that fox hunting is an expensive pursuit. One recent study estimates a regular participant in the hunt spends close to $25,000 a year for staff salaries, feed for horses and hounds, expenses for veterinarians, farriers, transportation, tack and equipment, buildings and fences, property taxes, clothing, and club dues. Interestingly, many passionate hunters are not at all wealthy, but are happy to sacrifice less-rewarding luxuries, like fast cars or fancy boats.

The object of the hunt is not so much the quarry as it is the chase itself—that unpredictable and thrilling factor that distinguishes all sportsmanlike hunting. It can happen only in a natural setting. Land development has forced some hunts to disband or relocate, but in other places in the American countryside, the presence of the hunt has helped to preserve the rural character of the surroundings for everyone.

"The end of the human race," predicted Ralph Waldo Emerson, "will be that it will eventually die of civilization." But in Saint Mary's County, Maryland, the direct descendants of Robert Brooke, Esquire, and strains of his original hounds are still hunting foxes.

IN THE BAR AT THE CHAGRIN VALLEY HUNT CLUB, A MURAL CARICATURES MEMBERS OF THE HUNT AS FUN-LOVING HOUNDS, DEMONSTRATING THAT AMERICAN FOX HUNTERS DO NOT ALWAYS TAKE THEMSELVES SERIOUSLY.

BLESSING OF THE HOUNDS

Bless, O Lord, rider and horse and the hounds that run in their running. . . ." So begins the traditional rite that opens fox-hunting season every fall for the Chagrin Valley Hunt of Gates Mills, Ohio. The ceremony—brief, formal, and rather touching—takes place on the front steps of Saint Christopher-by-the-River, an Episcopal church built in 1853, across the street from the hunt clubhouse.

Although other American hunts have since adopted the custom of the blessing, Chagrin Valley was the first to import it from England, in 1927. Townspeople turn out, rain or shine, to admire the horses and riders in their finest gray melton coats, buff breeches, and derby hats. Then the hunters load their animals on vans for the 30-mile trip to Amish farm country, where the club hunts now that the home grounds have become suburbanized. And they go with their blessings.

AFTER LEADING THEIR HORSES FROM THE HUNT CLUB TO THE CHURCH, *BELOW,* THE HUNTERS STAND IN SOLEMN ATTENTION, THEIR HORSES AND HOUNDS SOMEWHAT LESS INTERESTED, AS THE PRIEST PRONOUNCES HIS BENEDICTION. THEN ALTAR BOYS PASS OUT MEDALS OF SAINT CHRISTOPHER AND SAINT HUBERT (THE FRENCH PATRON SAINT OF THE CHASE AND OF CANINES) TO THE HUNTERS, WHO ATTACH THEM TO THEIR BRIDLES WITH GREEN AND YELLOW RIBBONS FOR GOOD LUCK.

HORSE AND HOUND HAVEN

Thorndale Farm in Millbrook, New York, has been in the same family for ten generations, and its houses, stables, kennels, woodlands, gardens, and fields bear the impress of each generation's particular agricultural bent and sporting passion.

Today, fox hunting, beagling, dressage, and Thoroughbred horse breeding are the principal focus on Thorndale's 600 acres, but the farm's unique and gratifying appeal may well be the way the checkered enthusiasms of the past and present share a position of respect and curiosity, alongside the calculated hopes for the future.

Thus, modern polo gear coexists peacefully in the main house with trophies of European hares dating

THORNDALE, WHICH BEGAN AS A MODEST, 500-SQUARE-FOOT SUMMER RESIDENCE, WAS EXTENSIVELY REMODELED IN GREEK REVIVAL STYLE IN 1850 BY JONATHAN THORNE, ONE OF THE MOST SUCCESSFUL MERCHANT PRINCES OF 19TH-CENTURY AMERICA, KNOWN FOR HIS "CLOSE HABITS OF INDUSTRY" AND PASSION FOR DRIVING FAST TROTTING HORSES. THE EAST WING OVERLOOKING THE REFLECTING POOL, ADDED IN 1901, WAS DESIGNED BY ARCHITECT THOMAS NASH. A FORMAL JAPANESE YEW GARDEN WAS CREATED ON THE GROUNDS TO COINCIDE WITH MILLBROOK'S HOSTING OF THE ANNUAL MEETING OF THE GARDEN CLUB OF AMERICA IN 1934.

THE PRESENT OCCUPANT'S EPONYMOUS GREAT-GRANDFATHER, OAKLEIGH THORNE, IS SHOWN IN HIS OFFICIAL HUNTING REGALIA, *BELOW,* IN A 1917 PAINTING BY RICHARD NEWTON, A GIFT FROM MILLBROOK RESIDENTS IN APPRECIATION FOR THORNE'S WORK IN BUILDING THE AREA'S FOX-HUNT TRADITIONS. THORNDALE, *RIGHT,* PORTRAYED HERE BY CHARLES H. HUMPHREYS OF CAMDEN, NEW JERSEY, WAS A STANDARDBRED STALLION WHO WON THE TROTTER'S PURSE AT FLEETWOOD PARK IN 1877.

THE HUNTER SHAMROCK, A FAVORITE OF ONE OF THE THORNE GIRLS, WAS PAINTED BY E. B. VOSS IN 1912. POLO IS THE PREFERRED EQUESTRIAN ACTIVITY OF THE OAKLEIGH THORNE WHO LIVES AT THORNDALE TODAY.

from the 1910s (when a pack of harrier hounds was first brought to the United States from England by an earlier Thorne). A new indoor riding ring, eminently practical yet pleasing to the eye, with its graceful Palladian windows, is a good architectural neighbor for the old cattle barn where the tack room is maintained. And in the venerable kennels on a distant hill, the beagles and basset hounds live together amicably.

More than 200 years old, Thorndale manages to breathe its history, heritage, and romance without wheezing, and that must be credited to Oakleigh Thorne and his wife, Felicitas ("Feli," for short),

FAVORITE PIPES, HATS, AND SPORTING PERIODICALS CROWD THE WORD SURFACE ON OAKLEIGH THORNE'S DESK, *LEFT,* WHILE J. M. TRACY'S 19TH-CENTURY OIL PAINTING DEPICTS A HUNTER AND BRACE OF POINTERS HOT ON THE TRAIL OF WOODLAND GAME BIRDS. ONE IN A SERIES OF LIMITED-EDITION PRINTS BY WILLIAM J. HAYS, *RIGHT,* SHOWS THE CULMINATION OF A DAY OF RIDING TO HOUNDS WITH THE MILLBROOK HUNT, OF WHICH FELI SERVES AS JOINT MASTER WITH FARNHAM F. COLLINS.

who handle the weight of all their tradition with grace, common sense, and great good humor.

Oakleigh caught a stocked trout with a worm on one of Thorndale's ponds when he was about five, and he has never stopped casting since. He says he'll fish "any time, any place," and family vacations "with fishing the major feature" have taken him to Nantucket, throughout the Rockies, and to the West Indies, where, he fondly reports, his son, Oakleigh, once caught an 85-pound tarpon on a fly.

A PAINTING BY HENRY ALKEN, *ABOVE*, RECALLS THE BETTING SPORT OF COCKFIGHTING, POPULAR IN COLONIAL TIMES. IN 1853, JONATHAN THORNE PURCHASED GRAND DUKE, *RIGHT*, PRIZE BULL OF THE FAMOUS BATES SHORT-HORNED CATTLE HERD IN ENGLAND, FOR $5,000 AND IMPORTED HIM TO AMERICA; GRAND DUKE'S PROGENY BECAME ONE OF THE MOST VALUABLE SHORTHAIR HERDS IN THE WORLD BY THE TIME THE HERD WAS SOLD TO WHITE SPRING FARM IN 1866. THE SHADOW BOX OF THE HOMESTEAD WAS A BIRTHDAY PRESENT FOR ONE OF THE 20TH-CENTURY THORNE MEN.

A BAVARIAN FARMER'S CABINET MADE IN BAD TÖLZ IN 1831, *LEFT,* DEPICTS THE FOUR SEASONS OF COUNTRY LIFE. FELI THORNE USED IT AS HER "PLAY CLOSET" WHEN SHE WAS GROWING UP; FILLED WITH CAMERAS, GAMES, AND TOYS, IT STILL SERVES ITS ORIGINAL PURPOSE FOR THE VISITING YOUNGSTERS IN THE KITCHEN AT THORNDALE. *ABOVE,* IMAGES OF BOTH SPORTING AND DOMESTIC ANIMALS, INCLUDING FISHES CARVED FROM SEMIPRECIOUS STONES, ARE A MOTIF THROUGHOUT THE HOUSE.

An active member of both the local Dutchess Land Conservancy and the national Trout Unlimited, Oakleigh observes, "I like the natural world, as undisturbed by humans as possible, and, in fishing, one can enjoy that environment and leave it almost as one found it," adding, "Even a well-fished stream has a touch of wilderness."

German-born Feli is an ardent horsewoman with an appreciation for horses that dates back to her first horse show "as a fourteen-year-old, totally out of control on my horse," she recalls, "and yet, thanks to that horse's efforts to please and do its best, I won a jumping class, and a bicycle!"

MARE AND FOAL, *ABOVE,* TESTIFY TO THE VIGOROUS THOROUGHBRED HORSE BREEDING OPERATION UNDERWAY AT THORNDALE TODAY. FELI THORNE CONVERTED AN OLD BARN INTO THE TACK ROOM, *RIGHT.*

THE FOX-HUNTING PRINTS OF THE NOTED EARLY-20TH-CENTURY ENGLISH ARTIST SIR ALFRED MUNNINGS ADORN THE WALLS OF THE TACK ROOM, *LEFT AND ABOVE,* COMFORTABLE AS AN OLD CLUB YET OPEN TO NEW IDEAS LIKE "VETERINARY ACUPUNCTURE."

As joint master of foxhounds for the Millbrook Hunt, Feli rides to hounds three times a week from August to December, but her interest in dressage, a demanding discipline that brings the precision of ballet into horsemanship, for both rider and horse, is year-round.

Like Oakleigh with his fascination with fly-fishing and the rigorous sport of polo, Feli takes her horses seriously. "My children would say that animals control my life, not the other way around," she declares, but is well aware of the benevolent family effects of life at Thorndale. "The unquestioning love and companionship of our animals helps to make Thorndale a real home," she says. "It's helped to teach our children early on about responsibility, consideration, and respect for the living creatures around them."

Thorndale got started in 1787 and the farm is only beginning to hit its stride.

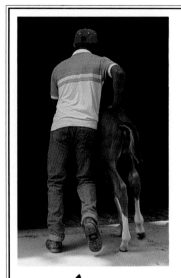

A SPRING FOAL, *ABOVE,* REQUIRES AS MUCH FRIENDLY SUPERVISION AS ANY RAMBUNCTIOUS SUMMER CAMPER. THORNDALE'S THOROUGHBREDS ARE STABLED IN A BARN THAT WAS ORIGINALLY BUILT FOR HUNTERS, *BELOW,* STILL BEARING THORNDALE'S HUNT COLORS OF DEEP GREEN AND RED. THE PAVING BRICKS OF THE STABLE, *RIGHT,* CONTAIN CORK TO CUSHION SENSITIVE HOOVES.

RIDING TO HOUNDS

Organized fox hunting, "a game played to rules whose origins are forgotten but still respected," in the words of an English enthusiast, has been enjoyed in America since colonial times. Today, there are more than 10,000 active participants in the sport, with about 150 foxhound packs registered with the Masters of Foxhounds Association in thirty-four states. For riders and spectators alike, the fox hunt is extraordinary rural pageantry. The athleticism of horses jumping timber fences or stone walls, the fervor of hounds as they close in on a scent, and the sight of a fox bolting for cover with what appears to be a grin on its face are some of the more arresting visual treats for observers at the spectacle.

Underlying the sport, which typically is mounted in the fall and early winter months, is a yearlong husbandry of land and animals that requires patience, dedication, and knowledge.

THE MILLBROOK HUNT, WITH HUNTSMAN BETSY PARK, *RIGHT,* IN CONTROL OF HOUNDS IN THE FIELDS, IS ONE OF THE OLDEST HUNTS IN THE COUNTRY, DATING FROM 1907. IT CHASES FOXES AND COYOTES ACROSS SOME 200 SQUARE MILES OF GRASS COUNTRY IN NEW YORK'S DUTCHESS COUNTY, WHERE STONE WALLS AND POST AND RAIL FENCES, *BELOW,* TEST THE METTLE OF BOTH HORSE AND RIDER. A "SPORTING" FOX MIGHT RUN TEN TO FIFTEEN MILES BEFORE "GOING TO GROUND"—TAKING SHELTER, USUALLY UNDERGROUND. IN A TYPICAL YEAR, THE MILLBROOK HUNT GOES OUT AS MANY AS NINETY TIMES FROM MID-AUGUST TO FEBRUARY.

AS PROFESSIONAL HUNTSMAN, BETSY PARK NOT ONLY DIRECTS HOUNDS IN THE FIELD BUT ALSO HANDLES THE CARE, FEEDING, AND TRAINING OF THE MILLBROOK HUNT'S PACK OF AMERICAN AND CROSSBRED FOXHOUNDS. HOUNDS ARE BRED FOR SCENT, VOICE, STAMINA, AND SPEED. THE QUALITY OF THE PACK IS MAINTAINED BY BREEDING THE HOUNDS EXHIBITING THE MOST DESIRABLE QUALITIES AND TRAITS EVERY YEAR, THEN TRAINING THE NEW PUPS TO KENNEL LIFE AND THE DISCIPLINE OF THE HUNT.

BENEATH THE OSTENSIBLY COMMUNAL LIFE IN A FOXHOUND KENNEL LIES A CAREFULLY STRUCTURED SYSTEM OF ANIMAL HUSBANDRY DESIGNED TO BRING OUT THE BEST IN THE DOGS (MALES) AND BITCHES. HOUNDS ARE TRAINED IN COUPLES, WITH PUPPIES PAIRED WITH OLDER HOUNDS DURING CUBBING SEASON, LEARNING BY IMITATION OF THE OLDER HOUND TO RESPOND CORRECTLY TO THE HUNTSMAN'S SIGNALS AND COMMANDS. AS TRAINING PROGRESSES, THEY ARE COUPLED TO HOUNDS THEIR OWN AGE, AND SUBSEQUENTLY ARE READY TO BE TRUSTED ON THEIR OWN IN THE FIELD.

THE HOME OF BEAGLING

The headquarters of America's most obscure — and, in some ways, esoteric form of the hunt is located at historic Institute Farm in Aldie, Virginia. The National Beagle Club, founded in 1889 to promote a new "foot sport" known as beagling, occupies what was once a part of Oak Hill, formerly the home of President James Monroe.

In 1916, the club took over the facility (from the estate of a family who had purchased it from the Loudon Agricultural and Mechanical Institute) and

its 500 surrounding acres of woods, meadows, and rolling farmland—ideal terrain for beagling, the pursuit of cottontail rabbits with trained packs of registered beagles and basset hounds.

The club's prime mover was unquestionably James W. Appleton, master of the Waldingfield Beagles of Ipswich, Massachusetts, America's first pack, founded in 1885 (and since relocated to Charlottesville, Virginia). Appleton was president of the club from 1892 until his death in 1942.

The earliest beagle trials were stag affairs, at Appleton's insistence, but by the late 1920s he agreed to let females on the property, although not exactly with the warmest of welcomes. He built a "squaw camp"—two board-and-batten cabins in the woods at a considerable distance from the club and the members' cabins.

A decade later, however, the squaw camp cabins joined the log ones and ever since then women have been as welcome as men, and have proved to be as skilled and as dedicated to what one enthusiast calls "the curiouser and curiouser sport of beagling."

ALTHOUGH THE CABINS FOR HUMAN VISITORS ARE NOT MUCH FANCIER THAN THE KENNELS FOR THE OUT-OF-TOWN PACKS, *BELOW,* EACH IS STAMPED WITH THE PERSONALITY OF THE PACK OWNER, AND FEW FAIL TO ACKNOWLEDGE AT LEAST TOKEN RESPECT FOR A FAVORITE QUARRY, *NEAR LEFT.*

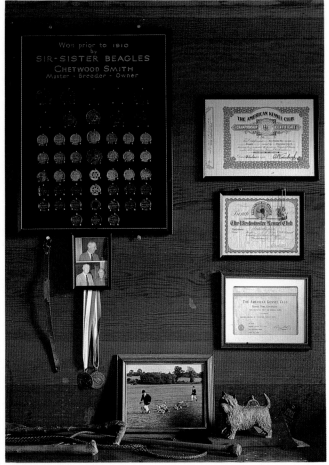

ATOP THE KENNELS, *LEFT,* A BEAGLE CHECKS WHICH WAY THE WIND IS BLOWING, ITS STERN (TAIL) AS ALERT AS ITS NOSE. PAST BEAGLING GLORIES, *BELOW LEFT,* ADORN THE WALL OF ONE OF THE PACK CABINS. THE MAIN ROOM OF THE CLUBHOUSE, *RIGHT,* EXUDES A LANGUOROUS SATISFACTION WITH ITSELF, UNDER THE DOLEFUL COLLECTIVE PAINTED GAZE OF CALYPSO, MARCANO, SERENO, LENTENOR, NICANOR, AND BARBARO.

APOTHEOSIS OF THE HUNT

Pebble Hill Plantation, Thomasville, Georgia, may well be the apotheosis of the sporting life in America, or close to it. Pebble Hill began as an ordinary antebellum cotton plantation, went into decline after the Civil War, revived around the turn of the century when a wealthy northern industrialist bought it, subsequently was destroyed in a fire, rose from the ashes, and was tottering along nicely as a winter hunting retreat, a kind of time-share Tara. Then along came "Miss Pansy."

Elisabeth Ireland Poe, who inherited Pebble Hill in 1936, was three persons in one, and all three sides of her character show up in her residence and on her grounds. She was an avid sportswoman who

NO MATTER WHAT ENTRANCE TO PEBBLE HILL IS CHOSEN, *LEFT,* THE LIKELIHOOD OF PASSING BY SOME REPLICA OF HORSE OR DOG IS HIGH. ONCE THE WINTER HOME OF THE HANNA FAMILY OF CLEVELAND, THE PLANTATION WAS DESTROYED BY FIRE IN THE 1930S, THEN REBUILT UNDER THE DIRECTION OF ABRAM GARFIELD, SON OF THE NATION'S TWENTIETH PRESIDENT, WHO EMPLOYED A TIMELESS ANTEBELLUM STYLE TO IMBUE HOUSE AND GROUNDS WITH ELEGANCE AND ROMANCE.

T HE LOGGIA, DESIGNED BY ABRAM GARFIELD TO CONNECT THE NEW HOUSE WITH THE STRUCTURE THAT SURVIVED THE FIRE, IS A WALK DOWN AN EQUESTRIAN MEMORY LANE, WITH PORTRAITS OF SOME OF AMERICA'S GREATEST RACEHORSES RENDERED BY NOTABLE SPORTING ARTISTS EDWARD F. TROYE AND F. B. VOSS.

A COLLECTION OF WALKING STICKS COMMEMORATES THE HUNT AND OTHER SPORTS AFIELD IN WHICH PANSY POE, THE [DOYENNE OF PEBBLE HILL] HERSELF PARTICIPATED AND EXCELLED: IN 1913, SHE WON THE NATIONAL HUNTER CHAMPIONSHIP AT MADISON SQUARE GARDEN. SHE MAINTAINED A KENNEL WITH OVER 100 FOXHOUNDS, SOME SETTERS, POINTERS, JACK RUSSELL TERRIERS, AND HER FAVORITE HOUSE DOG, THE GERMAN SHEPHERD.

not only loved fox hunting, shooting, polo, and showing hunters, but excelled at them. On one of her favorite horses, Sunrise, she won the national hunter championship in Madison Square Garden in 1929.

She also possessed rare taste and vision in selecting the treasures for her house, including oils and watercolors by renowned British artists, and works especially commissioned from American sporting artists Richard Bishop and A. L. Ripley. She hired Gene Pullen, a former engraver at the National Mint, to become her resident carver, and he made unique furnishings for her house and tack room skillfully imbued with equestrian and nature themes.

And she was a determined collector. You name it, Miss Pansy had more than one of it—stirrup cups, hunting horns, powder flasks, fox-hunt plates, sporting goblets, silver trophies, equestrian bronzes, porcelain horse figurines, and walking sticks.

Some visitors to Pebble Hill (open to the public since 1983, in keeping with the wishes of Mrs. Poe, who died in 1978) may find there is almost a surfeit of good things on exhibit here, but the main house has been kept exactly as Miss Pansy left it, and that makes it home.

THE TROPHY CASE IN THE "BIG ROOM" FEATURES DOORS INLAID WITH STYLIZED VIEWS OF THE FOX HUNT AND OF POLO BY A BOSTON CABINETMAKER. THE CARVED FINIAL OF A HORSE'S HEAD, *BELOW,* ANOTHER MASTERFUL GENE PULLEN CREATION, GIVES THE IMPRESSION THIS PROUD STEED MIGHT HAVE WON ALL THE TROPHIES HIMSELF.

ALBEMARLE
1969

L.J.L.H.S.
1966
CONFORMATION HUNTER, UNDER SADDLE
DONOR
THE MARTHA JOHNSTON SHOP
GIFTS – ANTIQUES

A LABRADOR
RETRIEVER CARVED IN BRONZE AND
A GOSSAMER SPIDER'S WEB, *RIGHT,*
FORM AN ARRESTING MORNING
STILL LIFE, WHILE A HORSE
NAMED CHINTZ, *BELOW,* BORN
A CENTURY AGO, LIVES ON IN
PEBBLE HILL PLANTATION'S
TENACIOUS MEMORY.

HUNTING IN VIRGINIA

The rolling hills, valleys, and woodlands of northern Virginia have long been considered the finest fox-hunting country in America, and one of the greatest concentrations of organized hunts is in this area. No single region better reflects the style and substance of the sport that two of our earliest Virginians, George Washington and Thomas Jefferson, also pursued with a passion. (Washington maintained a pack of hounds until his death.)

The oldest of the Virginia hunts is Piedmont Fox

THE HOME OF THE NATIONAL SPORTING LIBRARY, *RIGHT,* CONTAINS SUCH TREASURES OF FIELD SPORTS AS, *BELOW,* A. MUSS-ARNOLT'S PORTRAITS OF CHAMPIONSHIP HOUNDS; *POLO PLAYER,* A BRONZE BY CARROL BASSET; AND BEAUTIFULLY BOUND RARE BOOKS ON A VARIETY OF AMERICAN SPORTING PURSUITS.

Hounds, established in 1840 by Colonel R. Hunter Dulany, a legendary figure in fox-hunting circles who also founded the Upperville Horse Show in 1853. The Piedmont hosted the Great America Foxhound Match, a famous series of hunts in 1905 designed to settle the question of which was the better hound, the American foxhound or the English foxhound. (The American breed won the match, by a nose.)

The joint masters of the Piedmont today are Mrs. A. C. Randolph of Oakley Farm, Mr. Erskine L. Bedford of Old Welbourne, and Mr. Randy M. Waterman of Clifton Farm. Mrs. Randolph, a niece of General George Patton, once recalled hunting as a girl with the famous warrior as

A HORSEWOMAN'S ILLUSTRATED JOURNAL, *LEFT*, REVEALS THE YEAR-LONG FASCINATION OF EQUESTRIAN SPORTS; THE BOUND VOLUME OF *AMERICAN FARMER, BELOW,* IS TURNED TO THE PAGE WHERE APPEARED THE FIRST REGULAR SPORTING COLUMN PUBLISHED IN NORTH AMERICA, ON JANUARY 21, 1825. THE TROPHY ORIGINALLY WAS AWARDED TO ORACLE II, WINNER OF THE BETWEEN THE FLAGS STEEPLECHASE AT BELMONT PARK IN 1921.

"scary—he'd jump anything in front of him and you had to follow!"

"The Piedmont is definitely not a social hunt—our 'hunt breakfasts' are few and far between," Erskine says, noting that it is a challenge to serve as master of a hunt reputed to be the best or one of the best for over a century. "I just hope to leave it as great as I received it."

The idea of legacy and ennobling tradition is pervasive in Virginia's countryside. It is readily grasped in the Museum of Hounds and Hunting of Morven Park, or the exquisite grounds and gardens at Oatlands (site of the annual show of the Virginia Foxhound Club), or Vine Hill, a stately brick mansion at the edge of town in Middleburg. Built in 1806, this Federalist dwelling today serves as the offices of *The Chronicle of the Horse*, a weekly publication no serious horseman does without, and the home of the National Sporting Library, a rich

IN THE SERENE SETTING OF OLD WELBOURNE, *RIGHT,* THE FAMILY DEN, *BELOW,* REFLECTS WHAT COMES NATURALLY TO HORSE LOVERS IN VIRGINIA AND ELSEWHERE. THE PORTRAIT OF HORSEWOMAN LOUISE BEDFORD, ERSKINE'S MOTHER, WAS PAINTED BY FRANK VOSS. THE BRONZE SCULPTURE OF CORNELIA HARRIMAN GERRY, NANCY'S GRANDMOTHER, RIDING SIDESADDLE, *ABOVE,* WAS MADE BY C. C. RUMSEY IN ABOUT 1910.

archive of British, Irish, Canadian, and American books, magazines, and manuscripts on fox hunting and many other sporting pursuits from cricket to cockfighting. The library was founded in 1954 by Alexander Mackay-Smith, the curator, and George L. Ohrstrom, Sr., the owner of *The Chronicle of the Horse.*

One of the highlights of a tour of Middleburg is a visit to Journeymen, where Chuck Pinnell is likely to be making a riding boot for one of his customers, "the most complicated leather accoutrement worn by a rider," he asserts, "because the leg of a rider can be rendered functionally obsolete if the fit of the boot is not perfect."

Pinnell, who apprenticed in the harness shop at Colonial Williamsburg, first came to Middleburg in 1977, opened his own business the next year, and now has customers from all over the world. He also makes saddles, chaps, dog collars, belts, and other leather goods, but Chuck's boots are his most highly prized products.

FRENCH CALFSKIN FIELD BOOTS USED FOR INFORMAL HUNTS EARLY IN THE SEASON TAKE CHUCK PINNELL MANY HOURS TO BUILD. BEFORE CONSTRUCTION BEGINS, THE RIDER'S FOOT AND LEG ARE CAREFULLY MEASURED, WITH SUCH FACTORS AS HEIGHT, WEIGHT, AGE, AND FITNESS TAKEN INTO ACCOUNT. USING IMPORTED LEATHERS AND FITTING THE BOOT TO THE CUSTOMER FOR HEIGHT AND CIRCUMFERENCE BEFORE THE FINAL STAGE, PINNELL DELIVERS A PAIR OF BOOTS THAT FIT LIKE A GLOVE.

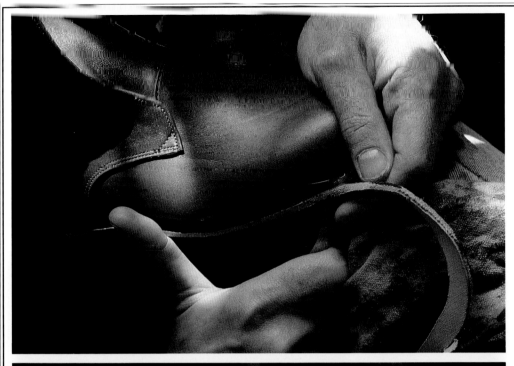

CHUCK PINNELL
DRIVES BRASS NAILS INTO THE HEEL
OF A PADDOCK BOOT BRACED ON
HIS JACK STAND, *LEFT,* AND USES A
CURVED AWL TO CUT STITCH HOLES
FOR THE MIDSOLE, WHICH IS THEN
HAND-SEWN. A STITCHING HORSE
AND THE CAMPBELL BOSWORTH
LOCKSTITCH SEWING MACHINE,
WHICH WAS INVENTED IN THE LATE
19TH CENTURY FOR MAKING
HEAVY STRAP GOODS, *ABOVE,*
ARE AMONG PINNELL'S HIGHLY
SPECIALIZED EQUIPMENT.

179

A STERLING SILVER
DOOR KNOCKER, *BELOW,*
DESIGNED BY THE OWNER,
BECKONS VISITORS TO A HOUSE
REPLETE WITH THE IMAGES AND
ACCOUTREMENTS OF THE FOX
HUNT, *RIGHT.*

FOXGATE

It's not just a pretty name for a house. The home of Barry and CeCe Kieselstein-Cord is called Foxgate because there really are foxes in the surrounding countryside, the site of what was once the largest potato farm in this region of upstate New York. The hounds and riders of the local hunt often bound through the property in search of them.

CeCe, a lifelong equestrian, has a special appreciation for the pageantry of the hunt and the inner workings and intricate commands needed by the hunt staff to control the field. Barry claims his own riding skills are not in CeCe's league, yet he enjoys the hunt and particularly relishes sharing early morning or late afternoon rides with her—"they're wonderful, calming, and romantic."

When the couple acquired the house (originally built in the 1700s), they removed the aluminum siding, ripped out extensive plastic to reveal the original woods, and restored fireplaces. Today, the rooms are full of images and icons of the hunt, many handed down from generations of horse lovers on

THE EARLY AMERICAN PRINTS DEPICTING THE CONTINENT'S FIRST HUNTERS ARE CHERISHED FAMILY HEIRLOOMS.

both sides of the family, others gifts from friends or unexpected finds in tack shops or antiques stores.

Barry, whose designs for jewelry, belts, and many other products have earned him international acclaim, has drawn on the countryside for inspiration for some of his work. "I've created a number of designs just from personal observations of animals, horses, dogs, and wildfowl," he says.

The natural world's impact on his family life is what makes Barry most grateful. "Watching our daughter grow in awareness and appreciation as the world of the outdoors unfolds before her has been wonderful," he says. "And when she caught her first fish, it was total bliss—that picture of her early childhood is forever etched in my mind."

AN EQUESTRIAN BRONZE, *ABOVE*, PRESIDES OVER A COLLECTION OF RIDING CROPS, INCLUDING OLD FAMILY PIECES AND SEVERAL DESIGNED BY BARRY KIESELSTEIN-CORD. THE LIVING ROOM, *BELOW AND RIGHT,* IS A COMFORTABLE GALLERY OF SPORTING ART, FEATURING ENGLISH AND FRENCH PRINTS WHICH CELEBRATE THE PAGEANTRY OF THE HUNT AND A COLLECTION OF ORIGINAL SILVER PIECES.

IN THE DINING ROOM, *RIGHT,* FURNISHED WITH ENGLISH AND AMERICAN ANTIQUES, A SERIES OF ANTIQUE BACHELOR HALL HUNT PRINTS FROM ENGLAND CONFIRM THE FAMILY'S PASSION FOR SPORT. THE PAINTING OVER THE MANTEL WAS COMMISSIONED AS A COVER FOR *FIELD & STREAM* IN THE 1940S. THE LANDSCAPE, *BELOW RIGHT,* ATTRIBUTED TO THE HUDSON RIVER SCHOOL, IS FLANKED BY A PAIR OF UNIQUE FOX HEAD SILVER SCONCES DESIGNED BY THE OWNER.

A 19TH-CENTURY PRIMITIVE AMERICAN FISH PAINTING HANGS ABOVE AN ANTIQUE ENGLISH CHEST, A STATELY WATERING HOLE COMPLETE WITH SILVER MINT JULEP CUPS BEARING THE LIKENESS OF A FAVORITE QUARRY, WHICH ARE ALSO THE OWNER'S WORK.

IN THE BEDROOM, WELL-READ BOOKS AND WELL-WORN BOOTS, *LEFT*, SPEAK TO ONE FAMILY'S PRINCIPAL SPORTING PURSUIT. THE FIREPLACE MANTEL, *OPPOSITE*, CONTRASTS THE STERN STUFF OF IRON HITCHING POSTS FROM THE 1870S AND IVORY-HANDLED BOOTJACKS WITH THE DELICACY OF AN ENGLISH BIRD PRINT.

THE LURE OF THE

"In Wildness is the preservation of the World," wrote Thoreau, and, he might have added, the salvation of the sporting life. For although many people may be motivated to fish and hunt for food, or pleasure, or social rank, without the factor of wildness there would be no sport, no climactic solitude, no apprehension of the unknown. The ancillary benefits of an expedition to the field, woods, or stream would, of course, become irrelevant.

Earlier generations of sportsmen took shelter in the wild in many forms, from humble lean-tos and shanties to majestic lodges and châteaus, or they came and went in stealth, leaving no trace. The surviving buildings still in use today tell the story of an ongoing passion for the natural

beauty and authenticity of the wild. The furniture is often rustic and rough-hewn, the porches are wide, and every room has a view. The working parts of the sporting life—the fly rods and shotguns and canoes and boats in so many distinctive re-

WILDERNESS

gional variations—have been crafted and maintained with obsessive interest. The trophies of the wilderness also come in many forms—some painted, hammered, and carved to last the ages. Others are simple examples of nature's boundless residue, a bird's nest or a sun-bleached skull brought back from a trek in the woods.

Wilderness is relative. Europe has been settled for so many thousands of years that the idea of the wild survives only in fairy tales. America's collective memory of wilderness is sharper. For the original colonists here, anything beyond the medicinal herb garden was terra incognita. As recently as the mid-19th century, as vast and inhospitable region as the Adirondacks was still largely unsettled and unknown except for a few intrepid hunters and guides. Today, at least within the continental United States, Wyoming and Montana are the sole surviving preserves of genuine wilderness, where the hunting ethic is an unquestioned part and parcel of daily life.

Snook Moore lives in the ruggedly beautiful Towsi Valley of the Bridger-Teton National Forest, a 26-mile drive, mostly over dirt roads, from the nearest town, Pinedale, Wyoming. Now seventy-five, he has spent half a century outfitting for big-game hunters, running some cattle, and more recently, feeding elk for the Refuge people. He is slightly bowed by age and the aftereffects of a dogsled accident a few years ago, but he has eyesight anyone would envy and a fierce sense of purpose that has made him a legendary figure in the mountains, recalling a time when everything in the West was larger than life.

Moore lost one of the outbuildings on his ranch to a fire in 1980, and in itemizing what trophies of his hunting prowess were destroyed he managed to evoke the bygone munificence of his surroundings. "An elk head with a 5-foot spread and 7 points each side, we lost," he recalled, "a 34½-pound lake trout, a pair of great deer and antelope, a tremendous big moose head, and a sheep fifteen years old—why just its horns and skull weighed 60 pounds—all gone up in smoke, exploding along with my canned goods. And if I was twenty-one years old again tomorrow, I couldn't put those creatures back. That's right, that size animal don't exist no more out here."

Carl Rungius, the German-born painter who became the Michelangelo of the big-game animals of the Rockies, made hundreds of solitary field trips into the rugged Wind River Mountains of Wyoming, often staying in the wild for four or five weeks at a time. "The advantage of being alone is that one man can get

CAMP UNCAS, BUILT IN 1893–94, OVERLOOKS A LAKE IN THE ADIRONDACKS WITH THE RUSTIC SPLENDOR ITS OWNER, THE BANKER J. P. MORGAN, EXPECTED.

much closer to his quarry than if he were accompanied by several others," he once explained in an interview. "I get more inside the life of my models when I go after them myself."

The animals Rungius killed were propped up on the spot in poses to simulate running, walking, and other actions too quick to capture by sketching from life. Then he would dash off a series of detailed pencil drawings from all angles. These were the basis for his finished paintings back at his studio.

Rungius was commissioned by the New York Zoological Society to paint some thirty canvases of vanishing American game between 1914 and 1934. The artist himself was well aware of wildlife population declines, both in numbers and in range. As early as 1904, reckless commercial hunting on a vast scale prompted Henry Fairfield Osborn, president of the Zoological Society, to assert in a speech to the Boone & Crockett Club, "Our animal fortune seemed to us so enormous that it never could be spent. Like a young rake coming into a very large inheritance, we attacked this noble fauna with characteristic American improvidence." He went on to plead, "It must not be recorded that races of animals representing stocks three million years of age, mostly developed on the American continent, were eliminated in the course of fifty years for hides and for food in a country abounding in sheep and cattle."

As our population swells, increasingly urbanized in outlook and cut off from the rural traditions of the nation, and as land development continues apace, the wild character of our unset-

BROOKS LAKE LODGE, STRADDLING THE CONTINENTAL DIVIDE IN WYOMING, CONTAINS A BIG-GAME TROPHY EXHIBIT REPRESENTING ANIMALS FROM SIX CONTINENTS.

tled forests, waters, and mountains becomes more elusive and, at the same time, more desperately desirable. *The Journals of Lewis and Clark*, that epic of the American wilderness, celebrated the flora and fauna of the New World even as it literally charted the way for a westering people to plunder it.

Two centuries later, we have the benefit of hindsight in recognizing the extraordinary heritage created primarily by sportsmen who understood the dynamic of the wild, and its eternal values, all along. "Hope and the future for me," said Thoreau, "are not in lawns and cultivated fields, not in towns and cities, but in the impervious and quaking swamps." Appreciation of the intrinsic value of "quaking swamps," along with fields, woods, streams, and all other manifestations of "wildness," is crucial to the ongoing struggle to preserve America's sporting life, and with it, America's remarkable natural heritage.

IN THE REMOTE AREAS OF AMERICA WHERE WILD GAME STILL LIVES IN PROFUSION, SPORTSMEN'S HOTELS AND LODGES ABOUND.

CENTRAL PARK HOTEL

GATEWAY TO THE GAMELANDS

MAINE FISHING CAMP

The great luxury is to have something with more than one generation to it," notes a longtime member of a Rangeley Lakes fishing club. Everything about this unique compound in the woods of western Maine confirms the imprint of older generations and the hope of younger ones.

Under the mute gaze of trophies of caribou and moose, the club's interior walls are layered with decades of humble reminders of the pleasures and intricacies of fishing and hunting in a wilderness setting. Old fly rods and fish mounts testify to early triumphs on lake and stream, and timeworn photographs preserve the resolute gaze and prodigious beards of beloved early camp guides and superintendents.

FROM THE VICINITY OF ELEPHANT MOUNTAIN, THE RANGELEY LAKES, *RIGHT,* STIR THE SAME REACTIONS OF AWE AND WONDER THE EARLIEST WHITE SETTLERS EXPERIENCED IN THE LATE 18TH CENTURY. SOME OF THE LAKES STILL RETAIN THEIR ORIGINAL INDIAN NAMES, SUCH AS UMBAGOG ("SHALLOW WATER") AND MOOSELOOKMEGUNTIC ("WHERE THE HUNTERS WATCH THE MOOSE BY NIGHT). VETERAN BOATERS, *LEFT,* ALWAYS TAKE ALONG THEIR SLICKERS, SINCE SUDDEN RAINSTORMS ARE A COMMONPLACE OF SUMMER.

THE VENERABLE CLUBHOUSE, *LEFT,* STILL SERVES AS THE SOCIAL CENTER FOR THE CAMP, ITS MANY TROPHIES RETELLING OLD FISHING TALES SUCH AS "LARGE ORNAMENTAL CHUBB, MAY 1954, NOTABLE BATTLE, WITNESSES." AN ADJOINING DORMITORY AND DINING ROOM ARE LARGELY IN DISUSE. UNTIL THE 1940S, A KITCHEN OPERATED FULL-TIME THROUGHOUT THE SUMMER MONTHS, AND UTENSILS, *ABOVE,* REMAIN BEHIND AS REMINDERS OF THAT SLOWER-PACED ERA.

The summer reading of a century ago can still be found on the bookshelves in such adventure titles as *The Tides of Barnegat, Belinda of the Red Cross,* and Zane Grey's *Riders of the Purple Sage.* Families arrived at the club by narrow-gauge railroad and lake steamer in those days and stayed the whole summer. Evenings, there were fires in the great fireplace and games of backgammon and Russian Bank, and someone could be counted on to wring a song or two from the cabinet organ.

Formed in 1868, the club is situated at the juncture of two rivers where they join the lake, with clapboard cabins known as "family camps" dotting the shore on both sides of the clubhouse. From the beginning, the club was determined to "preserve and protect" the fishing in the area. It built its own trout hatchery with breeding ponds. When salmon were introduced into the lakes in 1875, a second challenging game fish became available. Today,

populations and sizes of landlocked salmon and trout are not what they used to be, as the club monitors growing acidity levels in lake water and the potential effect of dams and other development on the health of a hauntingly beautiful but fragile ecosystem.

The club's first president, George Shepherd Page, was an avid angler who ran an investment business in Manhattan. He is credited with spreading the early fame of the Rangeley Lakes area when he showed some New York newspapermen the whopping eight-pound brookies he had caught on a trip in 1863. After press accounts of his catches appeared, city folk from New York, Philadelphia, Providence, and Boston soon descended on the area, and transformed a sparsely settled farming community into a major sport-fishing resort.

Today the great old wood-frame tourist hotels are gone, as are the mammoth fish, but on the Rangeley Lakes, devotion to the sport of fishing, its history, and its environment lives on.

Iₙ ONE OF THE FAMILY CAMPS, THE ARTISTRY OF A WOMAN FROM AN EARLIER GENERATION REMAINS ON THE WALLS, A TESTAMENT TO HER SKILLS WITH WATERCOLORS AND THE FISHING PROWESS OF HER FAMILY, *LEFT AND OPPOSITE.* BAROMETRIC CHARTS, *ABOVE,* WERE KEPT IN AN EFFORT TO CALCULATE WHEN FISH WERE BITING. IN THIS HOUSEHOLD EVEN A FISH OUT OF WATER, *RIGHT,* SERVES A PURPOSE.

THE RANGELEY BOAT, *OPPOSITE,* PATTERNED AFTER THE ADIRONDACK GUIDEBOAT, CAME INTO BEING IN THE 1800S, AND IT PROVED TO BE SO SEAWORTHY THAT ORDERS CAME FROM ALL OVER THE COUNTRY TO LOCAL CRAFTSMEN LIKE CHARLES W. BARRETT, BAKER TUFTS, AND H. W. LOOMIS. THIS ONE, ITS STERN SQUARED OFF TO ACCOMMODATE AN OUTBOARD MOTOR, IS PAINTED RED AND BLACK, THE COLORS OF THE FISHING CAMP. THE RUSTIC CHAMBERS REVEAL THE INDIVIDUALITY OF EACH MEMBER FAMILY, AS IN THE BATHROOM, *ABOVE,* WITH ITS FISHY CARICATURE OF THE OWNER, AND THE BEDROOM, *RIGHT,* WITH ITS UNEQUIVOCALLY STATED PHILOSOPHY: "THE WORST DAY OF FISHING STILL BEATS THE BEST DAY AT THE OFFICE."

THE MAIN
CLUBHOUSE, *RIGHT,* BUILT IN 1869,
IS SITUATED ON A POINT OF LAND
WHICH SERVED AS THE LANDING
FOR A STEAMER FERRY A CENTURY
AGO. DURING A WIND-DRIVEN
SUMMER HAILSTORM IN MAINE,
ABOVE, NOT EVEN A COVERED
PORCH PROVIDES MUCH REFUGE,
BUT WHEN IT ENDS, THE LAKE, *LEFT,*
ONCE AGAIN BECOMES AN OASIS
OF PERMANENCE AND SERENITY.

WHERE SALMON IS KING

Overlooking the Grand Cascapedia River, home water of the largest Atlantic salmon in North America, is Lorne Cottage, a place as evocative of sporting heritage as any on the continent. It was built in 1878 by the Marquis of Lorne after he married H.R.H. Princess Louise, fourth daughter of Queen Victoria, and moved to Canada in anticipation of becoming governor general. The couple discovered salmon fishing during a cruise on their yacht, which they would board every summer to escape the heat and stresses of Ottawa. The cottage changed hands several times until, 100 years later, another woman, Susan Engelhard, was in command, the equal of Princess Louise in poise and power of expression. In an elegant small volume called *Indian Summer* she writes of her compassion for the river, "not only in its natural beauty, but also in the beauty of what the river conceals, the life that is more than the life of the river itself."

A WEATHER VANE, *ABOVE LEFT,* MADE BY CAMP SUPERINTENDENT WARREN GILKER TOWERS OVER LORNE COTTAGE ON ONE OF CANADA'S MOST FAMOUS SALMON RIVERS, WHILE A TROMPE L'OEIL PAINTING BY A MEMBER, *OPPOSITE,* CATCHES THE EYE ON THE WAY TO THE KITCHEN. MR. AND MRS. THOMAS WILLETT, *RIGHT,* WHO PACKED ALL THE FISH CAUGHT IN THE RIVER IN THE OLD DAYS, ARE SHOWN WITH THE LARGEST SALMON EVER CAUGHT ON THE GRAND CASCAPEDIA, A 55½-POUNDER REELED IN BY A VISITING NEW YORK MAN ON JULY 17, 1939.

BUTTONED DOWN FOR WINTER, *OPPOSITE,* ITS FOOD CHESTS EMPTIED TO DISCOURAGE RAIDS BY BEARS AND OTHER MARAUDERS, LORNE COTTAGE WILL HIBERNATE WITH ITS STOREHOUSE OF SALMON FISHING IMAGERY. THE FIREPLACE, *ABOVE,* CEDES THE MAIN PLACE OF HONOR TO THE WOMAN WHO STARTED IT ALL, A "KEENER AND MORE PATIENT DEVOTEE OF THE SPORT THAN HER HUSBAND," ACCORDING TO ONE OBSERVER. "BORNE ON A FRAIL CANOE BETWEEN THE MICMAC INDIANS AND THE GUIDES, SHE EXHIBITED THAT INIMITABLE LOOK OF UNOBTRUSIVE BUT FEARLESS SELF-POSSESSION WHICH SHE DISPLAYED ON STATE OCCASIONS." OLD TROPHIES IN THE LODGE, *RIGHT,* TESTIFY TO THE RIVER'S EARLY ABUNDANCE. RECORDS SHOW THAT IN FOUR SEASONS FROM 1884 TO 1887, ONE FISHING PARTY ALONE TOOK 1,245 SALMON WEIGHING A TOTAL OF 29,188 POUNDS. DISASTER STRUCK IN 1953 WHEN DDT SPRAYING WIPED OUT ALL FISH, BUT SINCE THEN PROGRESS HAS BEEN MADE IN MAKING THE RIVER HEALTHY AGAIN.

43
L.D. AHL
JUNE 28 1924

42
M.P. KING
JULY 3 1922

FORGED-IRON HINGES IN THE LIKENESS OF SALMON AND A SALMON FLY USED AS A DECORATIVE DOORKNOB, *RIGHT,* THE WORK OF WARREN GILKER, GIVE CHARACTER TO A RIVERSIDE BUILDING USED TO HOLD FRESHLY KILLED FISH. OLD SPEARFISHING EQUIPMENT, *BELOW,* IS SCATTERED THROUGHOUT WARREN'S BLACKSMITH SHOP.

Warren Gilker, Lorne Cottage's legendary manager and guide for the past twenty-five years, is a third-generation blacksmith who forges weather vanes and door hinges in the likeness of salmon. "You can gauge the quality of the anvil by the ring it makes," he declared when a visitor stopped by his shop in a village of rural Quebec, and then crashed a hammer onto the very anvil with a mighty clang.

Gilker's handiwork adorns the fishing camp he runs as well as the houses of many of the guests who have passed through here. Among his other accomplishments are salmon smokehouse operator, former river warden, liaison man with the native Micmac tribe (he speaks their language), and collector and reader of books about salmon during the harsh winters, when the river freezes two feet thick. In summer, when the ashes in his smithy are cold, Warren whittles pliers to give away to friends. He makes about 200 pair a year, each fashioned from a single piece of wood, and never seems to have trouble finding 200 friends to give them to.

WARREN GILKER FORGES A CONE-SHAPED IRON PIECE, *LEFT,* TO PROTECT THE TIP OF A POLE TO BE USED FOR NAVIGATING ON THE GRAND CASCAPEDIA IN THE LONG CANOES USED FOR SALMON FISHING. OLD TOOLS MEANT FOR CUTTING BLOCKS OF ICE FROM THE RIVER EVERY WINTER, *RIGHT,* HAVE BEEN RELEGATED TO A WALL IN THE BLACKSMITH SHOP NOW THAT GASOLINE-POWERED EQUIPMENT IS AVAILABLE TO DO THE JOB.

CARVER OF FISH

Wilderness trophies come in many sizes, shapes, and forms, but there may be no single reminder of a day of pursuit more sublime and at the same time so friendly as a good fish carving.

Steve Smith, lifelong outdoorsman ("My parents said I spent my days sitting on the end of a dock, with a cane pole, when I was four"), professional musician (bassoon with the Chautauqua Symphony Orchestra), and devoted family man, first became fascinated with fish models years ago when he saw carvings made by John Tully for the Farlow Company in England.

"The idea of turning a trophy into a modest piece of sculptural art appealed to me," says Smith, a gifted draftsman and former bird painter. Since then he has made a specialty of rendering prize catches, particularly salmon, in tulipwood, carving the body of the fish down to its every scale, then painting in the color of its resplendent skin in a process so time-consuming he can only produce a half-dozen models a year in his Jamestown, New York, studio.

STEVE SMITH'S TROPHY CARVINGS OF SALMON, *ABOVE,* AND TROUT, *RIGHT,* ARE ARTISTIC RECORDS OF FISH, LESS ACCURATE ANATOMICALLY THAN TAXIDERMY VERSIONS BUT MORE PLEASING AESTHETICALLY. "THEY ARE VERY INDIVIDUAL," SAYS THE CARVER, "AND TEND TO REFLECT THE HAND OF THE ARTIST AS MUCH AS THE SPECIES OF FISH." SMITH'S PATRONS ARE USUALLY SPORTSMEN WITH A DEEP APPRECIATION FOR THE CRAFT TRADITION. "PEOPLE WHO LIKE TO LEARN ABOUT WHAT THEY COLLECT, WHO APPRECIATE CAREFULLY MADE THINGS, AND WHO LIKE TO TALK OVER HOW A THING WAS MADE OR USED," THE ARTIST SAYS, "ARE KINDRED SOULS TO ME."

MITH _23rd AUGUST 1987_ on "THE TWENTY-NINE" _Length 22"_

BRANDY BROOK

The salmon fishing lodges and hunting camps along the great rivers and rugged woodlands of Atlantic Canada are remote, "practically beyond civilization, beyond the din of life," as one early visitor put it, and Brandy Brook, on the Restigouche River in Quebec, is just such a place.

The lodge is named for a stream which empties into the Restigouche near the Home Pool. It was once owned by New York banker Robert Lehman, who entertained America's scions of finance and industry here. A New Jersey businessman rescued the lodge from ruinous decline a few years ago, repairing and modernizing the structure without altering its essential character as a kind of Old World log villa.

The sporting custom of catch-and-release is law on the Restigouche, and there are *gardiens de pêche* (fish wardens) to enforce it. That suits the tradition-minded occupants of Brandy Brook fine.

In the rod room in the center of the compound of buildings, *TOP LEFT,* are found the long rods and outsized nets, *BOTTOM LEFT,* required in the pursuit of salmon on the Restigouche. Visible from the lodge porch, *CENTER LEFT,* the home pool contains some of the largest salmon on the river, as entries in the log dating back more than a century will attest.

MOST FISHING ON
THE RESTIGOUCHE IS DONE WITH
HAND-CRAFTED SALMON FLIES, *FAR
RIGHT,* FROM BOATS WITH SMALL
OUTBOARDS ON THE SQUARED-
OFF STERNS, *RIGHT,* MOTORIZED
VERSIONS OF THE BIRCHBARK AND
DUGOUT LOG CANOES USED AS
LONG AGO AS 1840. STALKING
SALMON IN WADERS IS NOT
PRACTICAL BECAUSE THE POOLS
ARE DEEP AND A HOOKED FISH
WILL RUN GREAT DISTANCES. SEEN
FROM THE WATER, THE LODGE IS
AN IMPRESSIVE LOG VILLA, *BELOW.*

ADIRONDACK RETREAT

Some of the jewellike lakes of the Adirondacks have lost their glitter, their shorelines overtaken by densely built cottages and marinas. Not so Blue Mountain Lake, especially when viewed from the porch of Kla How Ya, a camp built by William West Durant, the creator of the Adirondack lodge style, in 1882. In that year, according to Harold K. Hochschild (a lifelong Blue Mountain Lake resident who wrote an exhaustive and fascinating history of the area called *Township 34*), the town was "the most fashionable highland resort in the northern states." Subsequent events, however, including an outbreak of typhoid fever, caused a precipitous decline in the hotel business.

WHEN THE EVER-CHANGING VIEWS OF LAKE AND SKY, *ABOVE,* FAIL TO CAPTIVATE, THERE IS PLENTY TO GREET THE EYE INSIDE THE HOUSE, *BELOW,* INCLUDING COLLECTIONS OF NATURAL AND MAN-MADE MATERIALS, THE OLD LEATHER MAIL POUCH FOR KLA HOW YA, AND A HUNTER IN FULL SKIRT.

THE LODGE, DESIGNED TO TAKE ADVANTAGE OF THE SURROUNDING NATURAL SPLENDOR, FEATURES A WRAP-AROUND PORCH, *OPPOSITE AND RIGHT,* AND AN INGENIOUS FLOORPLAN THAT PROVIDES EACH ROOM WITH THREE EXPOSURES. ALTHOUGH HE WAS NOT TRAINED AS AN ARCHITECT, WILLIAM WEST DURANT ACHIEVED AN APPEALING AMERICAN WILDERNESS RETREAT STYLE THAT WAS WIDELY COPIED THROUGHOUT THE COUNTRY.

Kla How Ya has been in the same family since 1923, and the family members' eclectic sporting interests, from fishing to fox hunting, are reflected in the rooms as vividly as their New York City roots.

Commuting regularly to town in a stylish old Chris Craft for food and supplies, the family enjoys Kla How Ya as it was meant to be enjoyed in the first place. They have never installed heating or electricity in the house, preferring fireplace warmth and the light from candles and kerosene lamps.

ONE FAMILY'S WIDE SPORTING SPECTRUM IS REVEALED IN THIS GLANCE FROM THE DINING ROOM, *RIGHT,* WITH ITS ANTLER CANDELABRA AND FOX-HUNTING TRIPTYCH, INTO THE LIVING ROOM, WHERE A MONSTROUS CODFISH, A 1920S FISHMONGER'S SIGN FROM FULTON FISH MARKET IN NEW YORK, LURKS ON THE FIREPLACE MANTEL CAMOUFLAGED BY LANTERN AND STONE. THE BIRCH SIDE CHAIR, *LEFT,* IS A NATURAL RESTING PLACE ESPECIALLY FAVORED BY SMALL CHILDREN.

THE WALK FROM THE
BOATHOUSE TO THE LODGE,
BELOW, IS STEEP, ESPECIALLY WITH
AN ARMLOAD OF GROCERIES, BUT
ALWAYS SATISFYING. IN THE LIVING
ROOM, ENUNCIATOR NO. 511
DATES FROM THE OWNER'S TERM
IN A SEAT ON THE NEW YORK
STOCK EXCHANGE.

CRAFTSMAN-MADE RUSTIC FURNITURE FROM THE SAME ERA AS THE HOUSE LENDS A SUITABLY RESTFUL NOTE TO ONE OF THE UPSTAIRS BEDROOMS. THE USE OF PEELED LOGS, BARK SHEATHING, TWIGGY TABLES AND CHAIRS, AND OTHER WOOD FORMS GIVES A MASCULINE BUT COZY CHARACTER TO AN ADIRONDACK LODGE, A FEATURE APPRECIATED ANEW TODAY AS PEOPLE SEEK TO FIND WAYS TO LEAD LIVES IN BALANCE WITH NATURE AND THE ENVIRONMENT.

BOATBUILDER JIM
CAMERON CUTS L-SHAPED PIECES
OF SPRUCE FROM TREES WHERE
TRUNK AND ROOTS CONVERGE,
BELOW, FROM WHICH HE WILL
OBTAIN THE RIBS WHICH GIVE THE
FINISHED BOAT, *RIGHT AND
OPPOSITE,* ITS NATURAL STRENGTH.
TO MAKE THE HULL LIGHTWEIGHT
YET DURABLE, HE PLANES QUARTER-
SAWN PLANKING BY HAND,
REMOVING THE WOOD IN
INFINITESIMAL FEATHERS, AND
THAT ALONE TAKES EIGHT HOURS
FOR ONE LENGTH FROM STEM
TO STERN.

A GUIDEBOAT MAKER

Twice as fast as a canoe, big enough to haul as much as 1,200 pounds, yet light enough to be portaged from pond to pond, the Adirondack guideboat is the product of the collective genius of the early mountain guides who lived in the Long Lake, Saranac Lake, and Raquette Lake area in the mid-1880s. Many of these guides were direct descendants of the Algonquians who first used the Adirondacks as their summer hunting grounds centuries before. Rather than slog through the nearly impenetrable forest, they devised a better way to carry their fishing and hunting parties into remote lakes and streams, with comfort, style, and dispatch.

Jim Cameron is one of a number of craftsmen carrying on the tradition of making guideboats by hand, in a workshop in the boathouse of a camp built in 1908, near Lake Clear. It takes about 400 hours for Jim to build a boat, from harvesting his own spruce, white pine, and cedar to fashioning the oars, paddles, yokes, and hand-caned seats and backrests. Some 4,000 brass tacks and 2,500 screws later, a guideboat representing the best of America's crafts tradition is ready for launch.

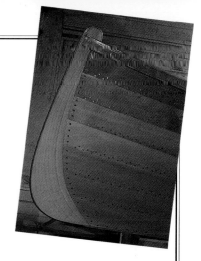

219

WILDLIFE ART SANCTUARY

The wilderness, much of it, hasn't changed as dramatically as we have," declares Bill Kerr, glancing up at the rugged Tetons from the steps of his sun-drenched log home, Moose Creek Ranch, in Jackson Hole, Wyoming. "Typically, we fly in to some remote location, burn some film through a motor-drive camera, and then fly out—returning to the unnatural world."

Over nearly three decades, Bill and his wife, Joffa, an artist herself, lovingly assembled one of the finest private collections of animal and sporting art in the country—which became the Wildlife of the American West Art Museum in Jackson in 1987.

But some of their favorites remain, enveloping Moose Creek in a rich and colorful tapestry of animals, nature, and the struggle of survival in the wild, including a small oil, *Pan Fish*, the first

The WYOMING RETREAT OF AN OKLAHOMA COUPLE WITH AN ABIDING INTEREST IN WESTERN WILDLIFE AND ITS DEPICTION IN ALL FORMS OF ART LIVES UP TO ITS NAME, NOT ONLY WITH REGULAR VISITS FROM MOOSE, BUT MULE DEER, BLACK BEAR, COYOTE, BADGER, PINE MARTEN, AN OCCASIONAL ELK, SQUIRREL, BLUE HERON, OWLS, AND ALL SORTS OF WATERFOWL AND OTHER BIRDS. THE KERRS ACQUIRED THE LOG HOUSE, BUILT IN THE 1930S, IN 1979 AND "WOULDN'T CHANGE IT FOR THE WORLD," BUT THEY HAVE FILLED IT WITH IMAGES ATTESTING TO THEIR KNOWING EYE AND PARTICULAR AFFECTIONS.

Trophy Mule Deer by Frank Hoffman is flanked on the left by two field sketches by Carl Rungius, the German-born "old master" of North American wildlife, who hunted and painted big game in the Rocky Mountains from 1895 until well into the 1950s. On the bureau, *Wild About Music,* sculpted by Joffa Kerr for the Grand Teton Music Festival, features a bear on bass, a coyote on violin, and a moose on oboe.

THE PORTRAIT OF A SKULL FOUND IN CARL RUNGIUS'S STUDIO IN BANFF, ALBERTA, WAS DONE BY KEN CARLSON AS A TRIBUTE TO RUNGIUS. THE WOLF, IN ACRYLIC, IS BY BOB KUHN, ONE OF THE PREMIER WILDLIFE ARTISTS WORKING TODAY. *APACHE* IS A BRONZE BY EDWARD FRAUGHTON. THE STAG PEERING OUT FROM THE BEDROOM WAS PAINTED BY ROBERT LOUGHEED.

painting in Bill's collection, a gift from Joffa when he was graduated from law school in 1962.

"The painting was intended as a reminder of our vacations at the family fishing camp in Minnesota with our children," Bill recalls. It was his father, former Oklahoma governor Bob Kerr, who had introduced him to the sporting life at an early age. "The whole family loved the picture, so before long we stopped by the gallery where Joffa found it. On that stop, we bought our first animal painting—of two mule deer in snow—and we were hooked."

Visits from animals in the flesh are one of summer's highlights on Moose Creek Ranch. The Kerrs' salt and mineral licks behind the house bring female moose with their spring calves. As Bill explains of his abiding affection for the West, "You can still be a part of much of what was here when the animals were the only permanent residents."

THE WINTER LANDSCAPE OVER THE FIREPLACE, *RIGHT,* SHOWS THE VIEW OF SLEEPING INDIAN MOUNTAIN THE KERRS ENJOY FROM THEIR FRONT PORCH. FLANKING IT ARE PAINTINGS OF A BLACK BEAR BY BOB KUHN AND MULE DEER BY ROBERT LOUGHEED. THE BRONZES ON THE MANTEL, SHARPLY CONTRASTING IN STYLE, ARE BY MELVIN JOHANSEN AND KEN BUNN. ON THE FAR WALL, THE DOMINATING IMAGE IS THE PAIR OF MOOSE IN *FIRST SNOW* BY CARL RUNGIUS TOWARD THE END OF HIS CAREER. JOFFA'S STUDIO, *ABOVE LEFT AND LEFT,* A FEW PACES FROM THE HOUSE, CONTAINS SEVERAL WILDLIFE WORKS IN PROGRESS.

A SCENE FROM THE TETON RANGE, PAINTED BY CONRAD SCHWIERING IN ABOUT 1980, HANGS ABOVE THE BED, *BELOW,* IN THE MASTER BEDROOM. THE VIEW OF LEWIS FALLS IN YELLOWSTONE PARK IN THE SPRING BY CONTEMPORARY ARTIST ROD GOBEL, *RIGHT,* OVERLOOKS TWO CLUB CHAIRS UPHOLSTERED WITH COLORFUL PENDLETON BLANKETS.

THE COMMERCIAL ILLUSTRATIONS OF FRANK HOFFMAN, ORIGINALLY USED ON CALENDARS AND GREETING CARDS, "A WHOLE SUBCULTURE OF ART," NOTES BILL KERR, LEND THEIR FRIENDLY PRESENCE TO MOOSE CREEK'S OFFICE. *A PRIZE TROPHY, LEFT,* DEPICTS THE SAINT MARY'S LAKE REGION OF MONTANA. THE BIRCHBARK MOOSE CALL ON THE WALL, *BELOW,* WAS USED BY INDIAN GUIDES IN THE LATE 19TH CENTURY.

DIRECTORY

SPORTING ART, ARCHITECTURE, CRAFTS, ANTIQUES, BOOKS, FURNISHINGS, AND FIREARMS

CALIFORNIA

Crane and Crane
11325, Unit F Sunrise Gold Circle
Rancho Cordova, CA 95742
(916) 638–2221

Sporting arms, accessories, and equipment.

Bob Marriott's Flyfishing Store
2700 West Orangethorpe
Fullerton, CA 92633
(714) 525–1827

Tal-Y-Tara
2103 O'Farrell Street
San Francisco, CA 94115
(415) 567–2881

Tack shop.

Kevin Williams
2450 Jefferson Avenue
Carlsbad, CA 92008

Traditional decoy carver.

COLORADO

Crystal Farm Antler Chandeliers
18 Antelope Road
Redstone, CO 81623
(303) 963–2350

Furnishings made from naturally shed deer, elk, moose, and fallow antlers.

CONNECTICUT

Eldridge Arnold
640 Lake Avenue
Greenwich, CT 06830
(203) 661–4352

Bird carver.

Chase, Ltd.
38 Grove Street
Ridgefield, CT 06877
(800) 229–9909

China patterns with fish and game themes. Call for the nearest retailer.

The Compleat Angler
2600 Post Road
Southport, CT 06490
(203) 255–3505

Tackle, books, and outdoor apparel.

David E. Foley
76 Bonnyview Road
West Hartford, CT 06107
(203) 561–0783

Sporting books.

John W. Oadlaw
7 Minjo Road
Danbury, CT 06811
(203) 790–4188

Bamboo fly rod maker.

Alan G. Haid
21 Outlook Drive
Darien, CT 06820
(203) 655–5188

Dealer, waterfowl and shorebird decoys.

Don Layden
21 Dorset Lane
Brookfield, CT 06804-1112
(203) 775–4103

Custom angling frames and three-dimensional mountings.

Mill River Fly Shop
3549 Whitney Ave.
Hamden, CT 06518
(203) 248–7850

Fly shop.

Chet Reneson
Tanturmorantum Road
Lyme, CT 06371
(203) 434–2806

Sporting artist.

Safari Outfitters
71 Ethan Allen Highway
Ridgefield, CT 06877
(203) 544–8010

Antique and new firearms, safari and hunting apparel.

Wildlife Gallery of New England
172 Bedford Street
Stamford, CT 06901
(203) 324–6483

Decoys, sporting and wildlife art.

FLORIDA

Sandy Proctor
P.O. Box 118
Monticello, FL 32344

Wildlife artist and sculptor.

GEORGIA

The Bookshelf
108 East Jackson Street
Thomasville, GA 31792
(912) 228–7767

Quail plantation titles.

Flint River Galleries
2662 Battle Overlook, N.W.
Atlanta, GA 30327
(404) 352–3606

Sporting books, art, and prints.

Foxfire Plantation & Hunting Preserve
P.O. Box 26
Thomasville, GA 31799
(912) 226–2814

Quail, pheasant, and other game-bird hunting.

Ron Hickman
P.O. Box 671004
Marietta, GA 30066
(404) 977–7998

Custom fly rod maker and guide.

George Stafford & Sons
808 Smith Avenue
Thomasville, GA 31799
(800) 826–0948

Manufacturer and outfitter in heart of quail country.

IDAHO

McCoy's Tackle Shop
P.O. Box 210
Ace of Diamonds Street
Stanley, ID 83278
(208) 774–3377

Fly shop, bird carvings in oldest building in town.

MAINE

L.L. Bean
Freeport, ME 04032
(800) 341–4341

Maine's main store for outdoor folk. Catalogue available.

John Bryan
39 Milliken Road
North Yarmouth
Pownal, ME 04069
(207) 829–6447

Woodworker and licensed Maine guide who specializes in carved fireplace mantels with fishing motifs.

Kittery Trading Post
Box 904, Route 1
Kittery, ME 03905
(207) 439–2700

Emporium for hunters, fishers, and campers.

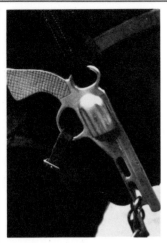

New England Arms
Box 278, Lawrence Lane
Kittery Point, ME 03905
(207) 439–0593

Antique and modern shotguns and rifles.

Richard W. Oliver
Plaza One, Route 1
Kennebunk, ME 04043
(207) 985–3600

Duck-decoy and fishing-tackle auctions and swap meets.

Stephanie and Don Palmer
Blueberry Hill Farm
Dallas Hill Road
Rangeley, ME 04970
(207) 864–5647

Antique fishing items, decoys, wildlife prints.

Lang's
31R Turtle Cove
Raymond, ME 04071
(207) 655–4265

Fishing-tackle auctions.

Sam and Jessie's Antiques
Box 71, Route 16
Oquossoc, ME 04964
(207) 864–5696

Down East sporting collectibles.

John Swan
61 Rosemont Avenue
Portland, ME 04103
(207) 772–1511

Sporting artist.

MARYLAND

Cap'n Harry B. Jobes
77 Baker Street
Aberdeen, MD 21001
(301) 272–2055

Chesapeake Bay decoy carver.

County Saddlery
2698 Jennings Chapel Road
Woodbine, MD 71797
(301) 854–6059

Tack shop.

The Sportsman's Den
2804 Dennis Avenue
Silver Spring, MD 20902
(301) 649–5740

Shooting, angling, and equestrian books.

MASSACHUSETTS

Christopher Cook
32 Phillips Street
Andover, MA 01810
(508) 470–0336

Artist.

Ted Harmon
2320 Main Street
West Barnstable, MA 02668
(508) 362–2766

Duck-decoy and bird-carving auctions.

Ralph Kylloe Antiques
Green Needles Road
Littleton, MA 01460
(617) 486–9756

Collectibles with sporting theme.

**Scott McDowell
Island Made**
12 North Water Street
Edgartown, MA 02539
(508) 627–5922

Silversmith on Martha's Vineyard specializing in hand-hammered models of bluefish, salmon, striped bass, swordfish, and skate.

Richard E. Oinonen
P.O. Box 470
Sunderland, MA 01375
(413) 665–3253

Angling-book auctions.

**Ken Reback
Sporting Antiquities**
P.O. Box 1395
Plymouth, MA 02360
(508) 746–8584

Sporting art and collectibles.

Snyder's Store
945 South Main Street
Great Barrington, MA 01230
(413) 528–1441

Rustic furniture, tramp art, and sporting trophies and mementos.

MICHIGAN

**Ron Fritz
Sporting Collectibles**
125 Morgan Street
Fife Lake, MI 49633
(616) 879–3919

Fish decoys.

MONTANA

Dan Bailey's Fly Shop
P.O. Box 1019
Livingston, MT 59047
(800) 356–4052

See flytiers at work, study Fishing Wall of Fame.

**Jonathan Foote
T-Square Ranch**
Box 4311, Route 85
Livingston, MT 59047
(406) 222–7800

Architect specializing in Western ranch designs and restorations.

River's Edge
2012 North Seventh Avenue
Bozeman, MT 59715
(406) 586–5373

Tackle shop.

Wade Gallery
116 North Main Street
Livingston, MT 59047
(406) 222–0404

Wildlife paintings and prints.

NEVADA

**Art Chesmore
Sporting Art Collectibles**
P.O. Box 26355
Las Vegas, NV 89126

Art and antiques.

NEW HAMPSHIRE

Stan Bogdan
33 Fifield Street
Nashua, NH 03060
(603) 883–3964

Custom salmon, steelhead, and trout reel maker.

North Country Taxidermy
Main Street
Keene, NH 19292
(518) 576–4318

Taxidermist.

NEW JERSEY

Carl Becker
37 Second Street
Fair Haven, NJ 07004
(908) 741–3488

Shorebird and decoy carver.

Bob Brown
273 South Main Street
Barnegat, NJ 08005
(609) 698–2718

Decoy carver.

Calderwoods Books
P.O. Box F
Long Valley, NJ 07853
(201) 876–3001

Sporting titles.

Spode China
(201) 846–1227

China with classic fox-hunt pattern "Herring's Hunt." Call for location of nearest retailer.

NEW YORK

Abercrombie & Fitch
Trump Tower, Level Five
725 Fifth Avenue
New York, NY 10022
(212) 832–1001

Reincarnation of the classic sporting goods store.

Adirondack Store and Gallery
Saranac Avenue
Lake Placid, NY 12946
(518) 523–2646

Antiques, paintings, prints, twig furniture.

American Bird and Crafts Studio
1 Main Street
Essex, NY 12936
(518) 963–7121

Decoys, bird carvings.

American Primitive Gallery
596 Broadway
New York, NY 10012
(212) 966–1530

Fish decoys.

Asprey
Trump Tower, Level One
725 Fifth Avenue
New York, NY 10022
(212) 688–1811

Antique silver jewelry and objects with hunting, shooting, and fishing motifs.

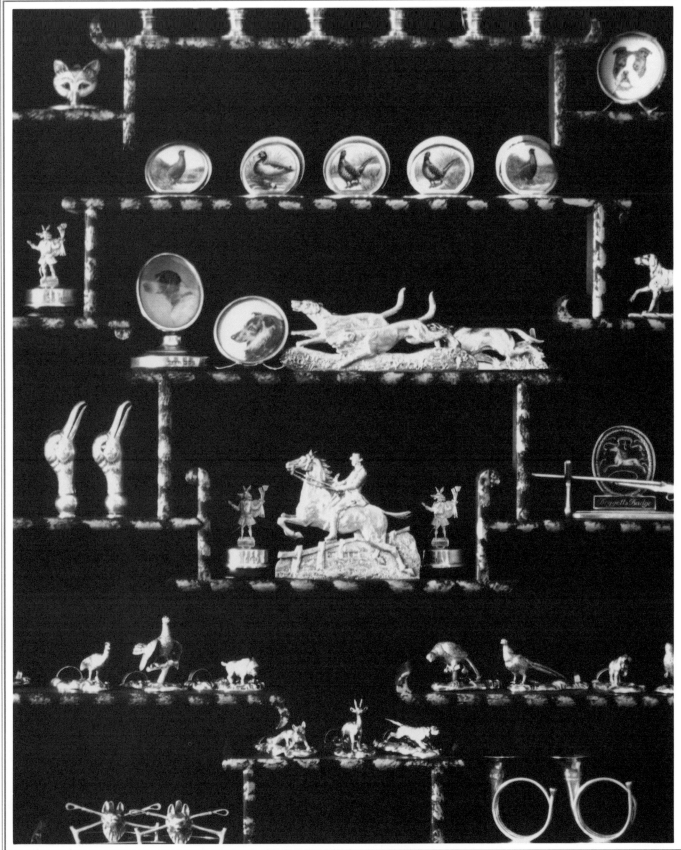

Barrett-Smythe
127 East 69th Street
New York, NY 10021
(212) 758–2225
Custom knifemaker.

The Bedford Sportsman
Depot Plaza
Bedford Hills, NY 10507
(914) 666–8091
Sporting gear and apparel.

Francis Betters
Adirondack Sporting Goods
Route 86
Wilmington, NY 12997
(518) 946–2605
Innovative flytier.

Michael Bird
Adirondack Design
77 Riverside Avenue
Saranac Lake, NY 12983
(518) 891–5224
Architect specializing in
Adirondack camp design.

Blue Mountain Lake Antiques
Route 28
Blue Mountain Lake, NY 12812
(518) 352–7668
Adirondack sporting antiques
and furniture.

Jim Bourdon
Nordica Drive
Croton-on-Hudson, NY 10520
(914) 271–3295
Dealer, fish decoys, lures,
and baits.

Judith Bowman
The Uncaged Woman
Pound Ridge Road
Bedford, NY 10506
(914) 234–7543
Angling, hunting, and natural-
history books.

Brunschwig & Fils
979 Third Avenue
New York, NY 10022-123
(212) 838–7878
Cotton and linen toile fabric
with hunting motif. Available
through designers.

Jim Cameron
Boathouse Woodworks
P.O. Box 317
Lake Clear, NY 12945
(518) 327–3470

Adirondack guideboat maker.

Hoagy B. Carmichael
Crosby Road
North Salem, NY 10560
(914) 277–8611

Bamboo fly rod maker and antique tackle dealer.

Walt Carpenter
P.O. Box 405
Chester, NY 10918
(914) 469–9638

Bamboo fly rod maker.

Peter Corbin
Shooter's Hill Press
Box 128-B, RD 1
Millbrook, NY 12545
(914) 677–9539

Sporting artist.

Covington Fabrics
Corporation
267 Fifth Avenue
New York, NY 10016
(212) 689–2200

Cotton fabric with hunt scene "Lawford." Call for nearest retailer.

James Cummins Bookseller
667 Madison Avenue, Suite 1005
New York, NY 10021

Sporting books and art.

Thomas Aquinas Daly
6365 East Arcade Road
Arcade, NY 14009
(716) 492–0846

Sporting artist.

Walter Dette
Cottage Street
Roscoe, NY 12766
(607) 498–4991

Flytier.

Walter H. Eissener
North Hillside Lake Road
Wappingers Falls, NY 12590
(914) 227–5933

Gunsmith.

Grand Central Art Galleries
24 West 57th Street
New York, NY 10019
(212) 867–3344

Sporting art.

Griffin & Howe
36 W. 44th Street, Suite 1011
New York, NY 10036
(212) 921–0980

Quality shotguns.

Grove Decoys
49 Grove Street
New York, NY 10014
(212) 924–4467

Bird and fish decoys and carvings.

Hathaway Boat Shop
7 Algonquin Avenue
Saranac Lake, NY 12983
(518) 891–3961

Adirondack guideboat maker.

Ken Heitz
Box 161, Route 28
Indian Lake, NY 12842
(518) 251–3327

Adirondack furniture maker.

Hèrmes of Paris, Inc.
747 Fifth Avenue, Suite 800
New York, NY 10151
(212) 759–7585

Sporting dog china collection "Chasse."

Hunting World
16 East 53rd Street
New York, NY 10022
(212) 755–3400

Adventurers' emporium.

Poul Jorgensen
Box 382, Cottage Street
Roscoe, NY 12776
(607) 498–5415

Salmon and trout flytier.

Barry Kieselstein-Cord
Bergdorf Goodman
1 West 57th Street
New York, NY 10019
(212) 753–7300

Jewelry designs, also available through Neiman-Marcus in Chicago and Beverly Hills and Mitsukoshi, Japan.

King Gallery
138 East 47th Street
New York, NY 10021
(212) 249–5010

Sporting and wildlife art.

Ron Kusse
Rena Marie Circle
Washingtonville, NY 10992
(914) 967–1876

Fly rod maker.

Ralph Lauren Home
Collection
867 Madison Avenue
New York, NY 10021
(212) 606–2100

Coordinated wallpapers and fabrics with fishing and hunting motifs: "The Sportsman's Collection"; hunt-inspired fabrics: "Kingsbridge"; and china with fox-hunt pattern: "The Berkshire Hunt." Available at all Ralph Lauren retail stores.

Tracy Law
The Curioddity Shop
14 West State Street
Shelburne, NY 13460
(607) 674–2375

Sporting books.

Allan J. Liu
American Sporting Collector
Arden Drive
Amawalk, NY 10501
(914) 245–6647

Fishing tackle, duck calls, and sporting books.

Maxilla & Mandible
451–5 Columbus Avenue
New York, NY 10024
(212) 724–6173

Animal and bird skulls and bones.

Northern Expressions Gallery
and Studio
Ferry Dock
Port Kent, NY 12975
(518) 834–2093

Hand-crafted wading staffs, Adirondack and Champlain Valley art and furnishings.

Thomas Phillips
Star Route 2
Tupper Lake, NY 12986
(518) 359–9648

Basket and twig furniture maker.

Jackson Levi Smith
Sagamore Conference Center
Raquette Lake, NY 13436
(315) 354–4303

Maker of Adirondack furniture, animal-head walking sticks.

Stephen Smith
47 Ellis Avenue
Jamestown, NY 14701
(716) 488–0139

Fish-model carver

Sotheby's
1334 York Avenue
New York, NY 10021
(212) 606–7000

Occasional auctions of sporting and wildlife art and antique firearms.

Shelly Spindel
1 Blackheath Road
Lido Beach, NY 11561
(516) 889–6889

Sporting art, books, and
collectibles.

Swann Galleries
104 East 25th Street
New York, NY 10010
(212) 254–4710

Occasional auctions of sporting art
and books.

Richard Tailleur
47-C Friar's Gate
Clifton Park, NY 12065
(518) 383–0068

Flytier.

Urban Angler
118 East 25th Street
New York, NY 10010
(212) 979–7600

Fly-fishing tackle shop.

PENNSYLVANIA

The Anglers Art
P.O. Box 148C
Plainfield, PA 17081
(800) 848–1020

Darryl and Karen Arawjo
P.O. Box 477
Sugar Mountain East
Bushkill, PA 18324
(717) 588–6957

Custom creelmaker to the stars
(Orvis, President George Bush,
and others).

**Dianna Dennis Bright
Bright Books**
P.O. Box 657
Unionville, PA 19375
(215) 347–9712

Beagling, fox-hunting, and
equestrian titles.

Sid Neff
524 Sycamore Road
Sewickley, PA 15143
(412) 741–3173

Flytier and bookbinder.

Dale D. Schoch
P.O. Box 403
Macungie, PA 18062
(215) 395–9216

Bamboo fly rod maker.

Mike Smyser
25 Broadway Avenue
Manchester, PA 17345
(717) 266–7294

Wood and cork decoy carver.

Steven Vernon
145 Ellis Road
Havertown, PA 19083
(215) 449–2887

Fishing tackle.

SOUTH CAROLINA

**Ambassador Graphics and
Wildlife Gallery**
3640 Ashley Phosphate Road
North Charleston, SC 29418
(800) USA–DUCK

Sporting and wildlife art, duck
stamp prints.

Robert B. Fraser
300 West Coleman Boulevard
Suite 104
Mount Pleasant, SC 29464
(803) 884–5717

Sporting and Southern art.

Robert M. Hicklin, Jr.
590 East Saint John Street
Spartanburg, SC 29302
(803) 583–9847

Sporting and Southern art.

TENNESSEE

Game Fair Ltd.
99 Whitebridge Road,
Apartment 105
Nashville, TN 37205
(615) 353–0602

Outfitter.

Scott Pilkington
P.O. Box 97
Monteagle, TN 37356
(615) 924–3475

Custom gun engraver and
knifemaker.

TEXAS

John Beck
9226 Landward
Houston, TX 77040
(713) 466–7102

Dealer specializing in fishing tackle
and ephemera.

Collectors Covey
15 Highland Park Village
Dallas, TX 75205
(214) 521–7880

Sporting art.

Crow and Company
2816 Ferndale Place
Houston, TX 77098
(713) 524–6055

Vintage sporting antiques and
appointments.

Brian McGrath
20005 Treehouse Lane
Plano, TX 75023
(214) 596–3293

Dealer, antique tackle, and
magazines.

Westgate Fabrics
1000 Fountain Parkway
P.O. Box 534038
Grand Prairie, TX 75053-4038
(800) 527-2517

Fabrics in the Fly-Fishing
Collection includes bamboo-rod
stripe, printed fly pattern prints,
and trompe l'oeil of fishing gear and
fish. Call for nearest showroom.

VERMONT

Johnny Appleseed Bookshop
Route 7A
Manchester, VT 05254
(802) 362-2458

Fishing and hunting titles.

Winston Churchill
RFD Box 29B
Proctorsville, VT 05153
(802) 226-7772

Custom gun engraver.

**Classic Outfitters and Fly
Fishing Shop**
Champlain Mill
Winooski, VT 05404
(802) 655-7999

Fly shop.

**Dr. Loy S. Harrell
Hawks Nest**
Hinesburg, VT 05461
(802) 482-2076

Decoys and other sporting antiques.

Fuat Latif
RDF 1, Box 20E
Orwell, VT 05760
(802) 948-2329

Canoe and boat maker.

Orvis
Route 7A
Manchester, VT 05254
(800) 548-9548

Home base for America's oldest
mail-order company. Catalogue
available.

Pierre's Gate
554 Main Street
Manchester, VT 05254
(802) 362-1766

Sporting art and carvings.

Horace Strong
RR 1, Box 675
Craftsbury Common, VT 05827
(802) 586-2575

Canoe maker.

VIRGINIA

The Hunt Scene
2 North Madison Street
Middleburg, VA 22117
(703) 687-6085

Equestrian art.

Murray's Fly Shop
P.O. Box 156
Edinburg, VA 22824
(703) 984-4212

Local pharmacy doubles as
outstanding tackle shop.

**Charles Pinnell
Journeymen**
16 South Madison Street
Middleburg, VA 22117
(703) 687-5888

Custom riding-boot and saddle
maker.

The Powder Horn Gun Shop
200 Washington Street
Middleburg, VA 22117
(703) 687-6628

Antiques and guns.

Red Fox Fine Art
7 North Liberty Street
Middleburg, VA 22117
(703) 687–6301
Animal and sporting paintings
and bronzes.

Russell Fink Gallery
P.O. Box 250
Mason Neck
Lorton, VA 22079
(703) 339–8684
Sporting, wildlife, and
equestrian art.

Saddlery Trade
115 Broad Street Road
Manakin-Sabot, VA 23103
(800) 446–7966
Tack shop.

The Sporting Gallery
11 West Washington Street
P.O. Box 254
Middleburg, VA 22117
(703) 687–6447
Paintings, books, and bronzes.

WISCONSIN

Fair Chase
P.O. Box 880
Twin Lakes, WI 53181
(414) 279–5478
Hunting, fishing, big-game, and
decoy books.

W. C. Russell Moccasin Co.
260 S.W. Franklin Street
Berlin, WI 54923
(414) 361–2252
Mountain hunting boots, hand-sewn
and custom-fitted.

WYOMING

Brooks Lake Lodge
P.O. Box 594
Dubois, WY 82513
(307) 455–2121
Historic lodge astride the
Continental Divide, with big-game-
hunting base camps.

Justin Bridges
Wind River Knives
P.O. Box 974
Dubois, WY 82513
(307) 455–2769
Knife maker.

Bill Davis
P.O. Box 50
Wapiti, WY 82450
(307) 527–7634
Sculptor of wildlife bronzes.

Ralph Faler
Hornhouse
P.O. Box 512
Pinedale, WY 82941
(307) 367–2452
Big-game taxidermist.

Jerry Fisher
P.O. Box 652
38 Buffalo Butte
Dubois, WY 82153
(307) 455–2722
Gunsmith and custom gunstock maker.

Flying A Ranch
Route 1, Box 7
Piwedale, WY 82941
(307) 367–2385
Guest ranch with spring-fed ponds for fly-fishing, vistas of Gros Ventre and Wind River ranges.

Marjorie Torrey
P.O. Box 794
Jackson, WY 83001
(307) 733–5344
Wildlife artist and sculptor.

Bob Wolf
P.O. Box 882
Wilson, WY 83014
(307) 733–9567
Wildlife sculptor and river guide.

CANADA

Atelier Fine Arts
588 Markham Street
Toronto, Ontario
(416) 532–9244
Decoys.

Avendale Antiques
1626 Bayview Avenue
Toronto, Ontario
(416) 487–4279
Decoys.

Warren Gilker
Grand Cascapedia
P.O. Box 33
Province of Quebec
GOC 1TO
(514) 392–4332
Blacksmith, salmon weathervanes.

R. G. Perkins and Son
Antiques
1198 Yonge Street
Toronto, Ontario
(416) 925–0973
Decoys.

SPORTING GUIDEBOOKS AND PERIODICALS

The Chronicle of the Horse
P.O. Box 46
Middleburg, VA 22117
(703) 687–6341
A weekly magazine in a newspaper format with fresh accounts of equestrian events held throughout the country, as well as articles on issues, ideas, and programs of special interest to horse owners.

The Collector's Guide to Antique Fishing Tackle
by Silvio Calabi
The Wellfleet Press, Secaucus, NJ
This large-format guide to old fishing equipment, illustrated with color photos, by the editor of *Rod & Reel* magazine, covers rods, reels, lures, decoys, art, and accessories.

Coykendall's Sporting Collectibles Price Guide
by Ralf Coykendall, Jr.
Lyons & Burford, New York
Designed to do for the sporting world what the Kovels' Price Guide has done for general antiques, this guide records the latest available prices, based on auction figures and catalogue offerings, for sporting prints, books, duck stamps, rods, reels, flies, plugs, fish and wildfowl decoys, firearms, and other sporting antiques and accessories.

The Decoy Geographer
4532 Old Leeds Road
Birmingham, AL 35213
(205) 967–8860
An annual guide to waterfowl decoy exhibitions, auctions, and museums in the United States and Canada.

Decoy Magazine
P.O. Box 1900 MBS
Ocean City, MD 21842
(301) 641–6084
Bimonthly for collectors of wildfowl decoys and other carved collectibles.

Gray's Sporting Journal
P.O. Box 130
Lyme, NH 03768
(603) 795–4757
A bimonthly magazine with photo essays on sporting topics, features showing the work of contemporary artists, and articles by sportsmen with an interest in literary expression.

Sporting Classics
1111 Broad Street
Highway 521 South
Camden, SC 29020
(803) 425–1003
A bimonthly magazine with columns focused on sporting art and collectibles, appreciative stories on contemporary sporting artists, and first-person accounts of exotic hunting and fishing trips.

Sporting Collectors' Monthly
RW Publishing
P.O. Box 305
Camden, DE 19934
(302) 678–0113
A classifieds paper for the collector, dealer, and investor in decoys, sporting collectibles, and wildlife art.

Spur
P.O. Box 85
Middleburg, VA 22117
(703) 687–6314
A glossy bimonthly with profiles of prominent equestrian families and farms, reports and features on equestrian spectacles, and articles on sporting art and collectibles.

FISHING SCHOOLS

Caucci/Mastasi Fly Fishing Schools
Box 102, RD 1
Tannersville, PA 18372
(717) 629–2962

Jack Dennis Flyfishing School at Teton Pines
Box 362-A, Star Route
Jackson, WY 83001
(800) 443–8616

Fishing Creek Outfitters
Box 310-1, RD 1
Benton, PA 17814
(717) 925–2225

Kaufmann's Fly Fishing Expeditions
P.O. Box 23032
Portland, OR 97223
(503) 639–6400

Letort Ltd.
P.O. Box 417
Boiling Springs, PA 17007
(717) 258–3010

Orvis
Manchester, VT 05254
(802) 362–3434
    and
166 Maiden Lane
San Francisco, CA 94108
(415) 392–1600

Joan and Lee Wulff Fishing School
Beaverkill Road
Lew Beach, NY 12753
(914) 439–4060

SHOOTING SCHOOLS

Griffin and Howe Shooting School
36 West 44th Street, Suite 1011
New York, NY 10036
(212) 921–0980

Holland & Holland
Sporting Clays Weeks
Vail Rod & Gun Club
Vail, CO 81658
(303) 476–5626

Orvis Shooting School
Manchester, VT 05254
(802) 362–3434

SPORTSMEN'S AND CONSERVATIONISTS' ORGANIZATIONS

Boone & Crockett Club
241 South Fraley Blvd.
Dumfries, VA 22026
(713) 221–1888

Ducks Unlimited
One Waterfowl Way
Long Grove, IL 60047
(708) 438–4300

Federation of Fly Fishers
P.O. Box 1088
West Yellowstone, MT 59758
(406) 646–9541

International Atlantic Salmon Foundation
P.O. Box 429
Saint Andrews, N.B., Canada
EOG 2XO
(506) 529–8889

International Game Fish Association
3000 East Las Olas Boulevard
Fort Lauderdale, FL 33316
(305) 467–0161

National Audubon Society
950 Third Avenue
New York, NY 10022
(212) 832–3200

National Wildlife Federation
1400 Sixteenth Street, NW
Washington, DC 20036
(202) 797–6800

Quebec Labrador Foundation
39 South Main Street
Ipswich, MA 01938
(508) 356–0160

Ruffed Grouse Society
1400 Lee Drive
Corapolis, PA 15108
(412) 262–4044

Trout Unlimited
501 Church Street, NE,
Number 103
Vienna, VA 22180
(703) 281–1100

Izaak Walton League of America
1401 Wilson Boulevard, Level B
Arlington, VA 22209
(703) 528–1818

Wildlife Action
P.O. Box 543
Mullins, SC 29574

Wildlife Legislative Fund of America
801 Kingsmill Parkway
Columbus, OH 43229
(614) 888–4868

SPORTING MUSEUMS AND LIBRARIES

FLORIDA

International Reference Library of Fishes and Museum
3000 East Las Olas Boulevard
Fort Lauderdale, FL 33316
(305) 467–0161

More than 8,000 books on fishes and recreational angling, plus a large collection of fishing films, videocassettes, and fishing-related photos.

GEORGIA

Pebble Hill Plantation
P.O. Box 830
U.S. Highway 319
Thomasville, GA 31799
(912) 226–2344

One of finest private collections of sporting art in the world; also stables, kennels, dog hospital, cow barn, and horse and dog cemetery.

Thomas County Museum of History
725 North Dawson Street
Thomasville, GA 31799
(912) 226–7664

Quail plantations, cotton plantations, hotel era, and other exhibits are contained in small but rewarding collection.

MARYLAND

Chesapeake Bay Maritime Museum
Navy Point, P.O. Box 636
Saint Michaels, MD 21663
(301) 745–2916

Decoys, sinkboxes, sneakboats, and various gunning skiffs.

Ladew Topiary Gardens and Manor House
3535 Jarrettsville Pike
Monkton, MD 21111
(301) 557–9466

A devoted fox hunter's historic house and grounds, including topiary hedges in the form of horse and rider chasing hounds.

Ward Museum of Wildfowl Art
655 South Salisbury Boulevard
Salisbury, MD 21801
(301) 742–4988

One of largest public collections of antique decoys, representing major waterfowling areas of the country.

MASSACHUSETTS

Addison Gallery of American Art
Phillips Academy
Andover, MA 01810
(508) 475–7515

Paintings, watercolors, drawings, and engravings by Winslow Homer.

Peabody Museum of Salem
East India Square
Salem, MA 01970
(508) 745–1876

Informative exhibit of Massachusetts decoy-carving traditions connecting waterfowl with species, boats, climate, and terrain.

MONTANA

International Fly Fishing Center
200 West Yellowstone Avenue
P.O. Box 1088
West Yellowstone, MT 59758
(406) 646–9541

Angling art, books, tackle, artifacts, and aquariums.

NEW YORK

Adirondack Museum
Blue Mountain Lake, NY 12812
(518) 352-7311

Regional museum of history and art, with exhibits on life, work, and sporting pastimes in the Adirondack region of upstate New York; over 450 paintings by Thomas Cole, A. F. Tait, Frederic Remington, and others. The library has 7,000 volumes and 60,000 historic photographs.

Catskill Fly Fishing Center
Box 130C, RD 1
Livingston Manor, NY 17258
(914) 439-4810

Flies, rods, reels, flytying desks, and other artifacts are on exhibit in area of nation's most historic trout waters.

Museum of American Folk Art
2 Lincoln Square
New York, NY 10023
(212) 595-9533

Exhibits often include fish and wildfowl decoy carving and other crafts related to sporting traditions.

New York Historical Society
170 Central Park West
New York, NY 10024
(212) 873-3400

Carved decoys and birds, extensive Audubon watercolors and Hudson River School landscape paintings.

Sagamore Hill
20 Sagamore Hill Road
Oyster Bay, NY 11771
(516) 922-4447

President Theodore Roosevelt's home, including the North Room filled with hunting trophies, books, and paintings, the Gun Room, and exhibits relating to the "Conservation President."

John L. Wehle Gallery of Sporting Art
Genesee Country Museum
Mumford, NY 14511
(716) 538-6822

Largest collection of sporting art in country—more than 600 paintings, prints, and bronzes spanning four centuries.

VERMONT

American Museum of Fly Fishing
Box 42, Route 7A
Manchester, VT 05254
(802) 362-3300

Abundance of treasures of American angling includes more than 1,000 rods, 400 reels, thousands of noteworthy flies, ephemera, and other rare or unique items; exhibits celebrate contemporary sporting artists, rodmakers, flytiers, and famous lovers of fishing, such as Theodore Gordon, President Herbert Hoover, and Ernest Hemingway.

Shelburne Museum
Box 10, Route 7
Shelburne, VT 05482
(802) 985-3344

Sprawling collection of Americana includes extensive decoy exhibits (nearly 100 Elmer Crowell miniatures), some fine sporting and wildlife paintings, re-created studio of artist Ogden Pleissner, and a re-created Adirondack-style big-game hunting lodge.

VIRGINIA

Museum of Hounds and Hunting
Morven Park
Box 50, Route 3
Leesburg, VA 22075
(703) 777-2414

Many exhibits on fox hunting, with paintings, drawings, prints, bronzes, maps, hunting horns, clothes, tack, books, and photographs.

National Sporting Library
P.O. Box 1335
Middleburg, VA 22117
(703) 687-6542

A research center for turf and field sports, their history, and social significances.

Refuge Waterfowl Museum
P.O. Box 272
Chincoteague, VA 23336
(804) 336-5800

Comprehensive collection of decoys and hunting artifacts; Delbert "Cigar" Daisey, resident carver.

WISCONSIN

National Fresh Water Fishing Hall of Fame and Museum
Box 33, Hall of Fame Drive
Hayward, WI 54843
(715) 634-4440

Spin fisherman's heaven: 5,000 classic fishing lures, 400 fish mounts, 300 classic and antique outboard motors, and "a walk-thru fish ½ city block long, 4½ stories tall."

Leigh Yawkey Woodson Art Museum
700 North 12th Street
Wausau, WI 54401
(715) 845-7010

Wildlife painting and sculpture.

WYOMING

Buffalo Bill Historical Center
720 Sheridan Avenue
Cody, WY 82414
(307) 587-4771

Extensive collections evoke "the real and mythic West through art and artifacts," including world's largest collection of guns, Plains Indian exhibit, and re-created Frederic Remington studio.

Wildlife of the American West Art Museum
P.O. Box 2984
Jackson, WY 83001
(307) 733–5771

One of country's premier public collections of North American wildlife subjects by artists ranging from the "Old Master" Carl Rungius, George Catlin, and George Russell to contemporary masters like Bob Kuhn and Ken Carlson. Outstanding temporary exhibits and educational programs.

CANADA

Margaree Salmon Museum
North East Margaree
Cabot Trail
Nova Scotia B0E 2B0
(902) 248–2848

Displays of old-time rods and tackle, books, pictures, and "poachers' paraphernalia."

Miramichi Salmon Museum
P.O. Box 38, Route 8
Doaktown, New Brunswick
E0C 1G0
(506) 365–7787

An aquarium stocked with salmon in various stages of growth, the replicas of a tackle shop and guides camp, a snow and ice house, and the polar opposites of hunting the king of fish: Poaching Corner and Salmon Hall of Fame.

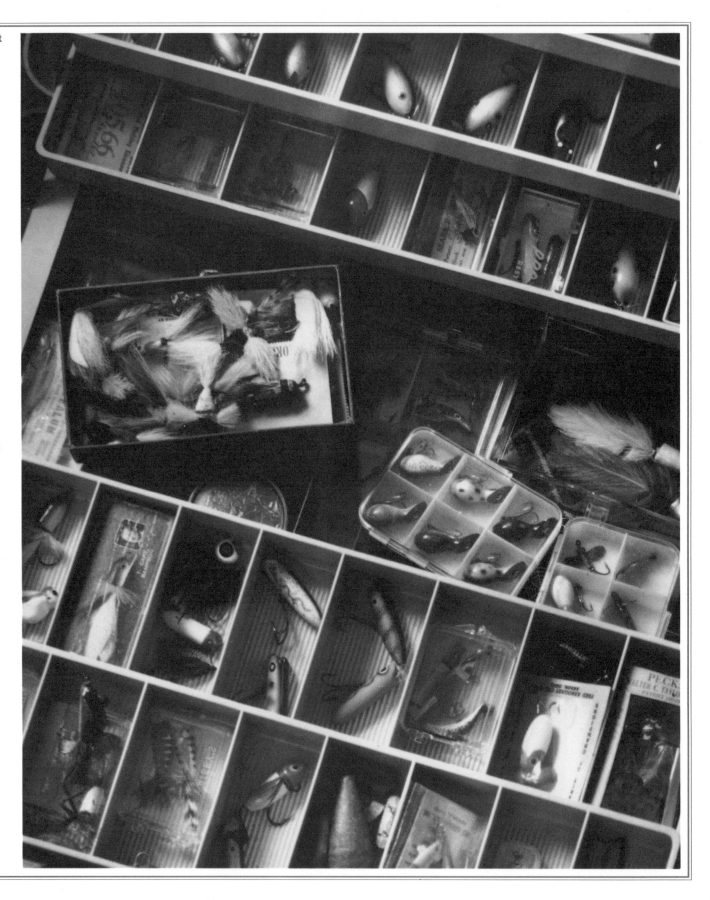